# A Shell Game

# A

# SHELL  Game

# A  SHELL

# GAME

With all best wishes Cécile E. Mactaggart

Cécile E. Mactaggart

ISBN 0-9699121-2-9

# CONTENTS

All of these shells were found dead.
Except for the Queen Conch, none
were collected alive.

## LIST OF ILLUSTRATIONS      Page

# FOREWORD

There is, inside us all, a savagery and cruelty which we try to sublimate as we grow older. The boy who picked wings off flies in his youth will often support the S.P.C.A. in his dotage. In between, he will have attempted to alleviate the sufferings of any warm-blooded animal that he encounters, especially if it can advertise its feelings by howling, crying, or shrieking.

It is otherwise with the cold-blooded kingdom which has no vocal cords. In spite of a wealth of scientific evidence to the contrary, as well as our own observation, we still subconsciously cling to the Victorian fallacy that fish do not feel. All skin divers know that fish are among the most sensitive creatures in the world, and any aquarium owner will tell you they have individual personalities. Yet when we catch them on our barbed hooks, we leave them to drown far more slowly in our environment than we would do in theirs.

The trouble is that we lack imagination. We do not extend our ability to put ourselves in the shoes of another, without which the Golden Rule is meaningless, beyond our own species. To some small extent, we look with disfavour on fur coats made from skins of wild animals that died slowly in steel traps or were clubbed to death as infants on the ice, but on the whole, we do not associate the beauty of the pelt with the ugliness of its acquisition.

Nowhere is this more evident than in collections of shells. Perhaps because they, themselves, are so breath-takingly beautiful, and so obviously inanimate, we make no connection with the soft, infinitely sensitive creature that required this armour as a shield from his environment. Yet, each one of these perfections of form and function represents a conscious act by the collectors to destroy a life usually in a manner more cruel than the worst excesses of The Inquisition.

As far as I know, this is the first book that has been written on how to enjoy the adventure of shelling without the killing. I recommend to you an author of some sensitivity. I hope that you will find her, as I have, an amusing and delightful companion in a new kind of shell game.

The Husband
of the Author
1988

# PREFACE

Finally I finished my book. Finally. I gave it to my children to read. "The best shell book of your lives?", I eagerly inquired on the day they turned the last page. This question they sidestepped with the ease of born diplomats, and instead subjected me to a hurricane of questions:

"What's a Dead Shell? What's a Live Shell? I've read this whole book, and I do not understand one single thing about dead shells or live shells."
"What's the Inside and the Outside? Inside and Outside what?"
"What's a Cut? What's a Bight? Why don't you have a map?"
"Who's Celine? I hate Celine. Can her. Get rid of Celine. This is a book about Shells, Mummy - shells, not Celine."
"What's all this *Uncle Tom's Cabin* stuff Mummy? We live in the modern age - no Uncle Tom slaves here. That kind of native talk is insulting to your readers."
"Why'd you write this book Mummy? You don't even tell the reason why you wrote it."
"Is this an idea for Jamaica or Cuba? What about Trinidad or Tobago? Why don't you say?"

" 'Jewfish'? Maybe they <u>used</u> to call them 'Jewfish' not any more Mummy, I can tell you."

" 'Fantasize about a 12" long True Tulip' from your collection?" Mummy, come on. That's sex. And you can't call 'operculums' 'Horny'. Think of another word. Pay attention, Mummy, **STOP LAUGHING!** You've got to consider your public."

"What are your credentials Mummy? **Who** are you? Where'd you come from? Your customers are going to need some logical coherence to this whole buildup of argument. Why should they listen to **you**? What gives **you** the right to expound **your** theories?"

\* \* \*

My father came from Boston. He had two brothers. The three of them decided on the wildly romantic adventure of buying Great Inagua Island from the Bahamian Government, making salt, and rapidly becoming billionaires.

My Mother came from New York. She was not used to outhouses full of cockroaches, flitguns for mosquitoes, freshly killed goat once a week, or screened-in larders whose legs stood in little tins of kerosene as protection against marauding ants. She was not used to lots of things, but she learned fast. Madly in love with my Olympian father, she rapidly gave him five children of which I was the eldest.

It was lovely - Inagua. For drinking we used to dip from out of a big pot in the kitchen. I can still see the battered, old, stainless steel dipper. I was twelve when my father built our first bathroom. It was very exciting having a real shower, almost as exciting as the bright red pickup truck he gave me that same year for my first job with my sister and my cousin: measuring the depth of the salt in the saltpans and taking rain gauge readings all over the island. The whistle blew at 6:00 a.m., 6:15 a.m. and 6:30 a.m. You had to be at work at 6:30 a.m. You knocked off at 4:30 p.m. You were big. You were an Adult. Adults had the funnest lives. You could sit with them at night while they drank their beer, and told their riveting stories.

**SHELLS**? Anybody was interested in shells? You must be kidding. Wentworth was my cousin. *He* did shells. Not me. I ran. I jumped. I swam. I swung in the swing. I climbed Ginep Trees. When I was bigger - 11 years old bigger - and had to go on voyages to Miami for straightening my teeth, I became Captain Bert Duncanson's right-hand man.

The night I was on the 10:00 p.m. until 2:00 a.m. watch, steering the Air Pheasant mailboat, and nobody came to check the course for four whole hours? The day one of the crew threw me my first 50 pound sack of flour from out of the hold, and I caught it all by myself? Those days? Still I hug them to me, dreaming secret dreams of remembering.

I didn't know I was fat and ugly. I didn't know anything except loving, loving, loving Inagua. And then the awful moment when I was 13 years old arrived. We were poor as church mice, instead of rich as billionaires. I had to go and get educated. I screamed. I wept. I cried. My parents were implacable. Education? Who wanted Education? Who needed it? I didn't mind being poor. Poor was fun, with 12 cousins and brothers and sisters all living in a huge old house with one Mother coming Up North for three months at a time. But **SCHOOL**??? Of all the awfulnesses I have ever endured, school was the worst. Not the learning part, but the learning-how-to-be-with-other-people-my-own-age part. Never before or since have I cried myself to sleep for so many nights in a row.

Luckily, when I was 19, my husband rescued me from my terrible misfortune. He was Lochinvar from out of the West, and he carried me off to Alberta, Canada, where I had to endure **NO MORE SCHOOL**. Faithfully, every single year, for 29 years, he brought me back to the Bahamas at Christmas time, so that I could recover my equanimity in the wide open spaces of my childhood. Not Great Inagua, now sold to the Morton Salt Company, but the Exuma Cays. I didn't mind. The Exumas were a radiant substitute.

Whether in the words of the *Yachtsman's Guide to the Bahamas 1993*, p.15:
> "Within a mere 50 miles of Florida's coastline lies entrance to the Bahama Islands, a 700-mile-long archipelago of pure crystal, bathed in the brilliance of perennial summer."

or in the earlier travelogue of J. Linton Rigg's *Bahama Islands*, 1949, p.xx,
> "Having gotten over to the British side of the Gulf Stream, the yachtsman will find a cruising paradise of unbelievable charm and beauty; crystal-clear water tinted by coral-pink sands, quiet beautiful harbors abounding in maritime life; good sailing breezes at all times, and probably the most perfect climate in the world."

it is hard to avoid hyperbole in describing the raptures of some of the Bahama Islands, and very particularly

## THE EXUMA CAYS.

Running for 100 miles NW to SE through the middle of the Bahamas, basically unpopulated, to me these cays represent every unspoiled wilderness. Most of the experiences in this book, and all of my shell collecting knowledge are derived from the time I have spent in these islands.

To answer the ill mannered criticisms from my family, and to lessen confusion on the part of a puzzled reader, here are a few

# DEFINITIONS

**INSIDE**
Inside this chain of cays, ie. to the West, is an immense, shallow Bahama Bank of sand covering hundreds of square miles. Stretching 60 miles to the Tongue of the Ocean this bank, called **THE INSIDE**, never exceeds a depth of about 20 feet, and its water is coloured aqua or turquoise or pale green. **INSIDE BEACHES** are apt to be calmer, not so windy, and more protected than Outside Beaches.

**OUTSIDE**
The low lying limestone cays themselves form the outer edge of this Grand Bank, (the retaining wall as it were, that keeps the sand from flowing away into the Atlantic Ocean), and only a half mile to the East of these islands the bottom drops sharply away to what Bahamians call "**THE EDGE**". Here it is thousands of feet deep, full of meandering sharks, and not a good place to practice swimming. This side of these islands is called **THE OUTSIDE**. It faces the prevailing winds, and as a consequence Outside Beaches are rarely as protected as Inside Beaches. Next stop Africa.

**CUTS AND BIGHTS**
There are spaces, or channels, between individual islands. Some are wide like Wide Opening. Some are narrow. All of them have water rushing in and rushing out every six hours. This rushing of waters is called **THE TIDE**. Tide is the flowing from ocean to

bank and back again, in an endless pendulum that raises and lowers the level of water twice a day by from 3 to 4 feet.

## LIVE SHELLS AND DEAD SHELLS
**A LIVE SHELL** has the animal who made its home still living happily inside. **A DEAD SHELL** has nothing inside. Either it is empty, or it is filled with dead, rotting, stinking animal.

## JEWFISH
*Fishes of the Bahamas* by Bohlke and Chaplin is considered **THE AUTHORITY ON BAHAMIAN FISHES.** Page 283 explains that the English name for Epinaphelus itajara Lichtenstein is Jewfish.

## CELINE
"And about Celine, Mummy?" Celine is a forest naiad. She dances under golden moons when the world is asleep. The whole of her life is ruled by "Want To". She's never on time because where she lives there isn't any time. She's very beautiful, and she's very shy. She never grows old. Her best friends are the winds in the Casuarina trees, and the stars at night. Lizards with blue curly tails share her lunch, and Banana Birds come to call. Celine spends her life doing important things like Poetry. She is never guillotined by Efficiency, or by being an Executive, or by Lists. February is Celine's writing month. During February Celine is always in residence in the Exumas. Celine is not Cécile, and Cécile is not Celine.

## WHY DID I WRITE THIS BOOK?
There aren't as many shells as there were five years ago, not as many as 10 years ago, and not nearly as many as 20 years ago. Why??? If you are one of the hundreds of boats cruising the Bahamas, **LOOKING FOR SHELLS** is a great pastime. **COULD IT BE A PASTIME WITH A DIFFERENCE**? Could it be **A NEW KIND OF GAME**? These are the questions which began to haunt me 15 years ago. In the beginning I was bedeviled with doubts. Would I be able to find proof for my argument? How could I write this book anyway when I was just a **BEGINNER**? Were Books for Beginners better written by Beginners? Says who? Who was going to play my game?

"People", answered Celine comfortingly. "People who can't run anymore. 'No more Jogging', their doctor said. They hate walking. Walking is so boring - no sweated Exhilaration, too slow. They need something to divert their minds, and keep them in shape at the same time.

Children could play it," continued Celine. "Children who were too little for Frisbee, children who the Big Boys wouldn't take Sailing, children who wished they could hold somebody's hand and go for a Treasure Hunt.

Sick people could play too, people who needed pick-me-ups, people whose worlds were coloured grey because they were so tired most of the time. Lots of people", murmured Celine hopefully to herself. So, "lots of people", here you are . . . .

With love from
Cécile  (Celine) Mactaggart
The Exumas
The Bahamas
February, 1989

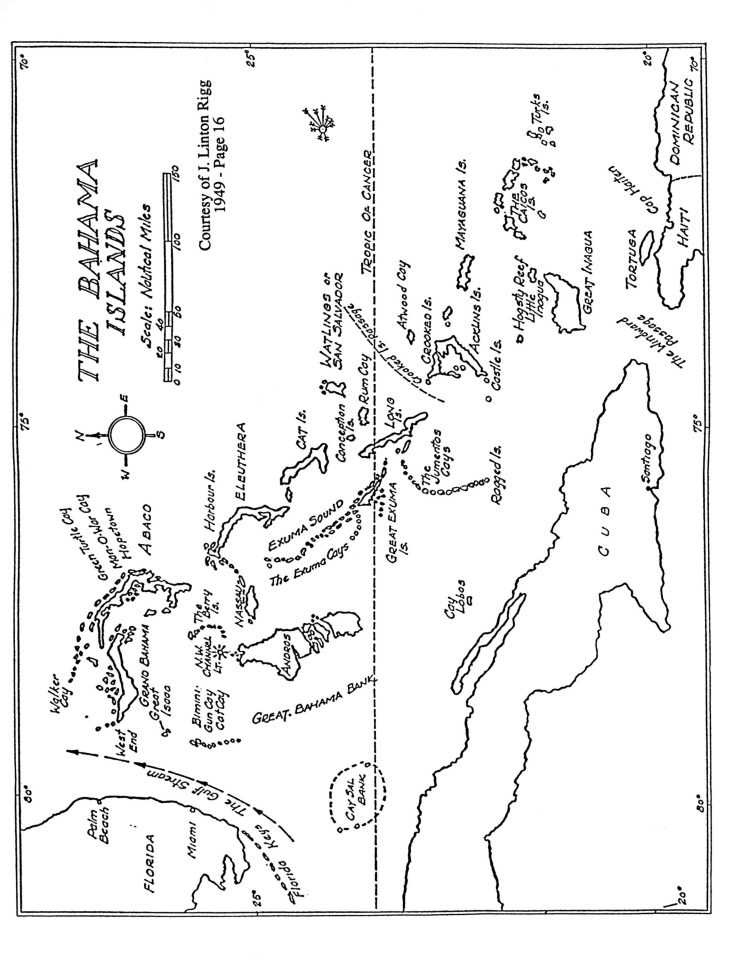

# THE BAHAMA ISLANDS

Scale: Nautical Miles

Courtesy of J. Linton Rigg
1949 - Page 16

# QUOTATIONS

"Some heavy snails may be 'hung' alive by tying the foot with string and hanging to an overhead branch.  The weight of the shell will gradually pull the snail free in a day or so."

*Seashells of North America*, p.42

"If you have a smooth, flat piece of wood or glass, tie your Chiton firmly to it in a flat position as soon as possible (after cutting him loose from its rock with a sharp knife).  Leave it until you are sure it has expired."

From a Book which sank to the bottom of the Sea in 1979, p.45

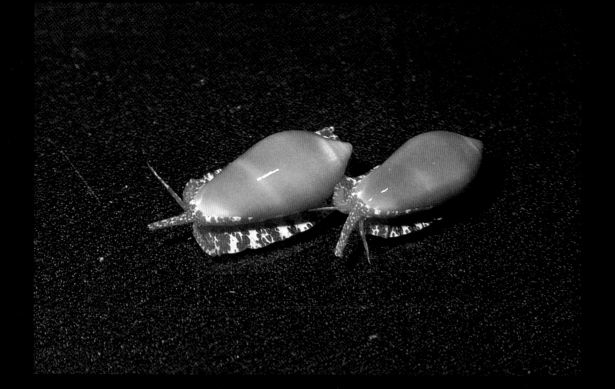

Twisting, turning, writhing, screaming, little eyes on ends of stalks wilting, mucousy slime dripping, "God, can you hear me God?" . . . But nobody hears the frantic screams from those cook house porcelains, bent hook twirling under the sun, string tied rigid to some crucifixion wood, warm sand scooped to bury alive . . . Nobody hears, and nobody cares . . .

# CHAPTER I

# A NEW KIND

# OF

# SHELL GAME

"I don't like all that."

"Me neither."

"Did you ever lie on your stomach underneath the water?"

"Once I did.  Remember?"

"It was all shallow.  Sunlight was filtering through the surface of the sea, turning the sand into golden squares."

"It was quiet.  You were pretending you could breathe underwater, just lying there, all still, with the light in golden squares."

"I was."

"Suddenly this old algae fossil began to move.  Out came his little head. Remember?"

"I remember."

"He had eyes on the ends of stalks.  His eyes looked all around.  They were interested in everything."

"He looked at me."

"He was only six inches away.  He could hardly help looking at you."

"I thought he was a rock."

"Yes, you didn't know about shells then."

"He wasn't a rock.  I thought, 'That's a funny kind of rock.  He moves.  He's got eyes and a head'."

"All of a sudden he started to nibble the under-water grass right near your fingers."

"He was grazing."

"He was a conch."

"Remember when you turned him over?"

"Oh - oranges and pinks and slurp he went right back into his shell, no trusting bright little eyes any more, just a horny kind of brown thing which snapped him right up shut, tight."

"Operculum.  That's called an operculum."

"And that beautiful, beautiful shell. You never would have suspected when you turned over that brown fossil rock how suddenly it could turn into such a beautiful conch."

"Conchs are Common."

"If there were only ten conchs in all the world, they would <u>not</u> be common. They would be rare. Bahamian Negroes as early as the 1700's, were calling this conch Queen. Queens in those days were important people, so they must have thought her very beautiful. Even Linnaeus in 1758, called her gigas which means giant, and everyone knows how powerful giants are."

"Let's play a new kind of game."

"Let's."

"Can anybody play?"

"Anybody."

"Let's just look for dead shells."

"But if we just look for dead shells, they're all chipped and cracked by the waves, dulled and faded by the sun - they'll be horrid."

"Says who?"

"Everybody. All the books tell you if you want **GOOD SPECIMENS** you have to collect them **LIVE**."

"Maybe all the books are wrong. People don't know everything. People used to think the world is flat. In 1957 they found a living fossil shell which scientists had scientifically maintained for years was extinct. Only they had made a mistake. It wasn't."

"If you knew how to look and where to look, maybe the scientists are wrong, like their books were wrong about the living fossil shell."

"Well your shells won't have those horny things."

"Operculums."

"Do operculums count?"

"For scientists they do."

"But for everybody else? - They're not scientists. Why do they have to collect shells the way scientists tell them to collect shells? Scientists make scientific collections for scientists. But nobody else has to. Everybody else can be different."

"Those scientist-made scientific ideas are using up all the shells in the world. Pretty soon there won't be any shells left. Shells will become extinct, all because scientists tell you that you can't collect beautiful specimens unless you collect them live."

"That's right. Kalahari Desert beaches with only old seaweed and tar is all we'll ever have. Who will like that?"

"Nobody."

"So what's our New Kind of Game?"

"Let's collect dead shells."

"What do you mean dead shells?"

"Let's collect them just **AFTER** the poor creature has died."

"Remember the day you saw a Tulip gobbling up a Netted Olive? It was low, low tide. The sand flats were stretching for miles, and there, underneath an overhanging cliff, a True Tulip was eating . . . "

"A shiny Golden Olive."

"Not nice for the Golden Olive."

"Maybe the Tulip anaesthetized him first with poison."

"Maybe."

"Anyway, you watched for hours. You came back the next morning to the same place. And guess what? No Tulip, but a precious Golden Netted Olive. Your first perfect Olive. No chips, no cracks, no fading, all shiny smooth."

"A Treasure."

"You can't always find Netted Olives being eaten up by Tulips you know."

"No, but during huge storms, if you walk and walk, sometimes, suddenly, you spy the perfect new kind of shell. Perhaps you had only ever seen him before in a book. It's so exciting. He's real. He's yours. You can add him to your tray."

"How do you know he's dead?"

"Because most times he's still inside.  He's rotting.  He smells foul.  The next tide's coming in soon.  Boiling waves are going to crack him and smash him.  But you found him first - before the tide changed.  Now, for years, every time you look at your shell, you remember the Casuarina trees bent double, the white foamed waves, the sand stinging your legs.  He's yours.  Anne Morrow Lindbergh called him *Gift from the Sea*."

"Show the scientists there are other ways to collect **A PERFECT SHELL**."

"Show the world."

"Maybe they're right about some shells - shells that live 70 feet under water or 200 feet. Perhaps then you <u>have</u> to collect live shells, and kill the poor animals inside."

"Perhaps."

"But maybe they're wrong about other shells - shells that you can find in shallow water - shells like Cockles and Tulips and Sunshells and Mussels and Helmets and Measled Cowries and Speckled Tellins and Sea Eggs."

"Hey get moving.  You better get moving."

"Hurry."

"Let's Hurry."

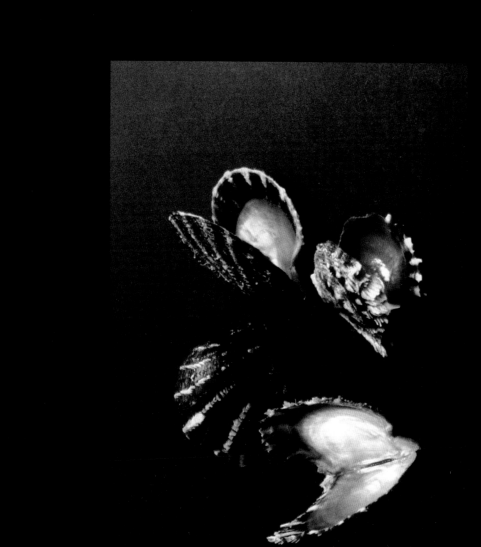

# CHAPTER II

# JOYS

# OF

To shell - to feel the sweet sunlight - to escape life's burdens - to breathe nature's revivifying air.

"Oh, I do think it the pleasantest thing
Ever a 'child' can do."

Walking is so boring.  Running is so exhausting.  Fishing, after the passing of years, makes one ask so many questions.

"It was the saying of Bion, that though boys throw stones at frogs
in sport, yet frogs do not die in sport."

Plutarch AD 46-120

Shelling is never boring.  Shelling is a perpetual Hunt for Treasure.  If you find none you can always secretly tell yourself you are going to find some tomorrow. If you find some, you can always drift home by the light of a sinking sun or a rising moon, bemused and enchanted with your unexpected luck.  Why you?  Why is this your day?  Sometimes you even have to stop your boat, unscrew your container, just to look again, just to make sure the beauty you found all by yourself is truly still there.

Most mornings when you awake and you are in the Exumas, there is a grace and charm, there is a colour of light - the sand is so white, the sea is so green, there seems no alternative but to greet the day with a pent-up, Hallelujah shout of,

"Let's go shelling".

Andrew Wyeth once wrote that if he painted all of his life in Pennsylvania or Maine, still, all of his life would not be long enough for him to really know Pennsylvania or Maine.  Me too.  All of my life would not be long enough for me to really know the Exumas.

Collecting Shells . . . Collecting Memories . . .  No sheller ever forgets the delicious circumstances surrounding his first Real Treasures.

On the morning I picked up my first Flamingo Tongue, and, at that exact second a baby Osprey flew by, clutching a newly caught fish, and beating his wings to escape collision with a newly excited sheller - I can forget that morning?

The Full Moon evening I happened to glance down at my feet lost in a dream called Stars Twinkling in Mirror Smooth Water and . . . a perfect Long-spined Star Shell?  They really existed?  I held it to the moon in awe.  I had never seen one before, except in a book.

Oh Treasures of Shells - and the reason you never forget any of them or their surroundings?  Every time you pick one up you remember the day, the time, and how your feelings of frustration, crossness, and weariness suddenly turned into elated exhilaration.

# CHAPTER III

# RULES

# OF

"Beach shells, however, are only simple husks, lacking their softer parts, and often worn by the action of water and sand. Bivalves are often missing a valve. Anyone who wants to devote himself seriously to collecting soon begins to search for living specimens..."

*Guide to Shells*
Bruno Sabelli, p.45

The only possible exception to Never Ever following this advice is the Bahamian Queen Conch discussed in the last chapter of this Book.


## RULE #1 - LIVING SHELLS ARE OUT

The more you begin playing this New Kind of Shell Game, the more likely your interest will quicken. Nothing is more heavenly than to read books by learned gentlemen assuring you of the impossibility and the impracticability of building a significant dead sea shell collection, when that is just what you are doing.

Every single time you find a perfect, brilliant, and unchipped, unmarred-in-any-way specimen, you can gleefully say to yourself, "Hum . . .". With perseverance and dedication, your dead shell collection might one day rival many a museum's live one.

"Not for operculums. Not for rigid, scientific data."

"No. But for Perfection, and Beauties singing Songs of Radiance . . . Yes."


### Breaking Rule #1 By Collecting Just One Live Shell

Don't. Or you're not allowed to play. Look at your matchless find with its perfect living creature inside for as long as you like. Hold him to the light. Cover him in cool water. Wait for a few hours. Come back to look at him again. And again. Admire his shine. Swoon before his perfect curve of lip. Orange Rooster-tail Conch, magnificent Reticulated Cowrie Helmet, Tulips as big as feet, the only Triton in my life: I can still remember Satan, urging me in all his glory, towards my first Foul Deed after I had already invented this game.

Don't.


## RULE #2 - PUT BACK ROCKS

Many shell collectors think that shells lie under rocks and perhaps this is true. However, while acting upon this information, it is sad if you turn over a rock with a casual toe, or a mighty hand, find nothing under the rock, and then walk blithely ahead, whistling a little, unconcerned song. If you practice this often, there are some who will mutter "Murderer" under their breaths as they pass you by, their disdaining eyes causing your skin shivers of harm . . .

Crabbies and other squirming, interesting sea creatures live under rocks. If you leave a rock the wrong way up, all the eggs, (which are sometimes attached to its underside), will never grow into adults. Schools of fish will nibble away at those nice, fresh, living organisms. Above the water-line, scorching sun will burn, causing just as certain havoc and destruction.

When you become tired of turning over rocks, you can stop. All shells do not live under rocks.


**RULE #3 - ONE SHELL A DAY**
used to be my motto. You can collect fifty, but only one of your fifty may be fine enough for your finest tray. The others can be used for gifts, or study, or for interest. Year after year, I watch my Interest Tray grow, and, year after year, it becomes more interesting. But my Interest Tray is not my Beauty Tray.

My latest motto is One Shell a Week. This is because I have been looking for twenty years. If you are just beginning to collect, One Shell a Day should last you several years.

I am only talking about **PERFECT SPECIMENS**, and I am only interested in Perfect Specimens. I may have one or two Imperfect Specimens in my collection, but that is because they are waiting for the right tide, the right time, the right place, and the right storm to be replaced.

If you are like my Mother, who loves shells for all their magic whirls and twirls, and who often thinks chips or breaks add interest to her collection - you can have a very beautiful other kind of collection, just as rewarding to you as mine is to me. All collectors establish rules for anything they collect. My rules involve Perfection. Your rules might involve Shine or Colour or Shape. Aside from my Rule #2 about **PUTTING BACK ROCKS**, the only unbreakable rule for this game is **NO LIVE SHELLS**. This is the kind of game where the more skillful you grow, the more rules you can invent for prolonging your anticipation and excitement.


**RULE #4 - DON'T CHOOSE YOUR BEST SHELLS UNTIL ALL OF THEM ARE DRY**
Each evening all of us who play this Shell Game rinse out our day's finds in a bowl of fresh water, and lay them to dry upon paper toweled trays or plates. The next morning we rush to see what we can see, and often stand, sadly discourged, because, the next morning our shells are dry. Dry shells are hardly ever last night's beauties. They have changed from heavenly, shining first-borns to dull, scratched-by-the-sand discards. Upon finding Treasure, it is better to warn oneself with, "Wait-and-See" than to suffer, unsuspecting, a too dreary sense of loss twelve hours later.

You need never worry about a Beauty Shell. Under the water, on the sand, on a tray, the day before rinsing, the day after, it will always shine with perfection. It is just that until a Beauty Shell is <u>completely</u> dry you cannot tell into what sad or happy category it is going to fall.

Of all these gay deceivers Sunshells are the worst. When they are wet from the ocean you are so positive of "promised joy". The next day, far too often, you are throwing them back into the deep, humming wryly to yourself for comfort a little Gilbert & Sullivan.

> "Things are seldom as they seem
> Skim milk masquerades as cream."

## RULE #5 - TAKE CARE OF CUTS

In the Bahamas if you do not take care of cuts, the infections sure to torment you will feel like hot, scurrying around ants eating you up alive. The tropics have peculiar revenges for those who are heedless.

If your cut is small, drip drops of Hydrogen Peroxide into it with a wet Q-Tip until every single piece of sand comes foaming out. Sometimes a needle helps. Once the cut is free of sand, Neosporin and a bandaid will do the healing trick. If you decide a cut on your foot is too trivial to warrant this kind of attention, and it becomes badly infected, soaking it in very hot water is a more laborious and much more painful necessity.

**BAD CUTS** are a different matter altogether. If you are having nightmares about Gangrene and can hardly look at your foot, you have a bad cut. Staying off it for a day, and keeping it high upon a cushion will aid the healing process. During your first few times of hobbling around beaches, you might wear rubber Booties or taped up garbage bags. Silver tape is the best. Perhaps you should give up the beach. Whatever you do - do not give up soaking.

There is no way **A REALLY DEEP CUT,** which should have had stitches, is going to heal in less than three weeks. Even when these cuts are new and uninfected, we soak them in hot salt water for half an hour every morning and night - just in case. After 27 years of playing doctor, I have decided major cuts heal faster if you do not remove their flaps of skin. It is all a question of how careful you are in cleaning out every single horrid particle of sand.

If your cut is on your foot and after it is **POSITIVELY CLEAN**, you may bind it up with Neosporin and some bandage from a roll of Elastoplast. One of those nice Johnson & Johnson two inch bandaids feels lovely, but Elastoplast adheres better.

## RULE #6 - MEDICINE CHEST ON BOARD THE MOTHER CRAFT

Last but not least, wise players of this New Kind of Shell Game will have these Medicine Basics waiting to greet them at the end of each day's weary exploring. When needed, these items, or similar substitutes, are needed badly, and not just by shellers. Even surfers or divers might come begging a loan from such forehanded supplies.

**Q-TIPS** have a lot of uses.

**HYDROGEN PEROXIDE** - Wetting a Q-Tip so that your Hydrogen Peroxide drips into cuts works miracles at foaming out grains of sand.

**NEOSPORIN** is a favourite antibiotic cream for travelers to the Exumas.

**BANDAIDS** of different sizes for large cuts and scrapes are a must.

**BAND-AID PLASTIC STRIPS** by Johnson & Johnson two inches wide seem invented especially for wounded feet.

**ELASTOPLAST FABRIC DRESSING STRIP** which never comes off unless deliberately peeled is even better. But since this is made in England it is often difficult to find.

**STERILE PADS**, a couple of boxes of different sizes are a fine substitute for elastoplast.

**TAPE**, adhesive and Dermicel First Aid Cloth Tape by Johnson & Johnson will be useful when you are applying your sterile pads.

**SCISSORS** - the large size orange ones by Fiskar are a fabulous investment. Their brilliant colour makes them hard to lose.

**ANTIBIOTIC PILLS** for stinging coral infections which become infected are nice to have on standby.

**POISON BUSH AND INSECT BITE MEDICINE** - Two good sprays are Decaspray by Merck Sharp Dohme and Topisolone by Hoechst Ireland Limited. A spectacular ointment for Poison Bush from England is Synalar Gel by Imperial Chemical.

**EAR DROPS** - Cortisporin otic solution (Polymyxin B, Neomycin Hydrocortisone) is a very effective brand for bad ear infections.

**MEAT TENDERIZER** - People say that if you are ever slashed by a Sting Ray, or stung by a Portuguese Man of War you will wish you had some Meat Tenderizer handy to rub into the burning, itching areas of your skin.

**A CANDLE**

**AND SOME MATCHES** - You can find out about by reading p.53.

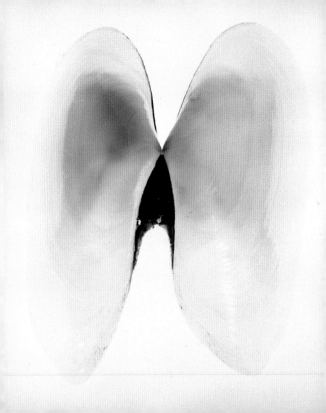

# CHAPTER IV

# NAMING

When I was at the beginning of the beginning, lost and bewildered amidst the seeming millions of South Pacific shells, it seemed to me whenever I attempted to pin down just one of these unfamiliars, Linné would appear.  Linné 1758.  Linné 1770.  "Linné was a man?",  I asked myself?

Linné <u>was</u> a man I decided, with hawk eyes and a beard, intrepidly sailing to all the strange corners of the world.  He was Darwin and the "Beagle", but earlier than Darwin and the "Beagle", and therefore braver.  More daring, and even more full of curiosity than Darwin.  Naturally Linné became my Hero.

Every day he collected specimens, risking his life upon wild, strange reefs.  If he judged the tides incorrectly, crashing waves and devouring sharks awaited his first miss-step.  Every evening, even during howling storms, he would descend to his creaking cabin.  While candles guttered in their candlesticks, he would think, and dream, conjuring Names for Shells from out of the romantic ether.

When he found himself holding a particularly beautiful shell, realizing he was about to name it for all time for all mankind, up to the deck he would climb.  There, pacing backwards and forwards, beneath a golden moon slow rising from the sea, he would seek divine inspiration.

Alas for the romance of dreams.  The real Linné's "pursuit of excellence" included far greater horizons than sailing the Seven Seas.  Born Carolus Linnaeus in 1707, he died in 1778, during his lifetime becoming one of the world's and Sweden's greatest naturalists.  Aside from teaching and studying medicine and botany, and aside from being ennobled Karl von Linné in 1761, he was most famous for his 180 scientific volumes which included the *Systema naturae*, 1735 and the *Genera plantarum*, 1737.  These two works began the **BINOMIAL SYSTEM OF NOMENCLATURE** still in use today.

Maybe Linnaeus never collected shells.  Whether he did or not, collectors sent them to him from all over the world, so that with his new system he could invent new names.  I like to think of him as being so horrified at receiving a jumbled description of a "marbled Jamaican murex with knotty twirls" that he then and there divided up the whole animal kingdom into phyla.  Imagine his satisfaction when he labeled once and for all this "Marbled Murex", (my particularly adored Bahamian Queen Conch), Strombus gigas Linné 1758.

**LINNAEUS' RULES**
Linnaeus' Binomial System of Nomenclature has about as many rules as my Shell Game, only they're more difficult to remember.  He says that the first name - the general or generic or group name - in other words the <u>genus</u> name is ALWAYS CAPITALIZED.  This name always comes first.  Strombus gigas Linné 1758 is first of all a Conch or Strombus.  Next he has a special or specific name which applies just to him - in other words the <u>species</u> name - his very own name, gigas or Giant.  This name always comes second.  Strombus gigas shares his gigas with no other Strombus in all the world, and gigas always starts with a little letter.  The species name or second name, is NEVER CAPITALIZED.  If, as beginners, we

occasionally want to feel ourselves in the rarefied air of true science, we walk along the beach bowing to all our attendant royalty murmuring,

"Good morning, your highness Strombus gigas Linné 1758."

We add the name Linné after Strombus gigas because we know that the name of the <u>author,</u> or person who first described our conch, comes after our conch's two part scientific Latin name, often with the actual year during which its christening took place.

Names change. Don't despair.

> "Seeing an old favourite with a new name often gives collectors a feeling of sadness and frustration," said one of the sympathetic authors in my bibliography.

Shell names change because of all the information which keeps pouring in. My only thanksgiving is that some beautifully sounding names which have taken me years to memorize:       Cyphoma gibbosa
Janthina janthina
Spirula spirula
    and      Laevicardium laevigatum
have not changed in the last 20 years.

Naming shells is the most difficult chapter in this book. My idea is that people will not read it unless they become really hooked by this game. Scientists write in a manner difficult for Beginners. I have read this information at least one hundred times, and still my comprehension is slow. Even when I consider this chart:

## NAMING A SHELL

for example

### The Queen Conch

(pp. 117, 118)

| FIRST NAME | SECOND NAME | THIRD NAME | DATE |
|---|---|---|---|
| **Strombus** | **gigas** | **Linné** | |
| The Genus name. Many other shells have this name. Many other shells are conchs or strombuses. Always capitalized. | His very own name. His specific name. No other conch shares this name. No other conch is a gigas or Queen conch. In Latin it is never capitalized. | The name of the person who first described this shell. | The date of this description. Sometimes it is not known. If it is, a comma precedes it. |

still it is hard for me to comprehend each new year when shelling begins again. What I can comprehend is Linné. Doctor, teacher, lecturer and scientist who wrote 180 volumes of science. It boggles the mind imagining his quill pen scratching through the night - some lives holding so many lifetimes, others barely able to encompass one.

## PHYLA

There are about thirty phyla in Linnaeus' well ordered animal kingdom. A Phylum is a group of Living things with similar anatomies. Shells belong to the Phylum Mollusca. This Phylum is the second largest of all the Phyla. Some people state that it comprises more than 100,000 species. I cannot imagine learning the names of 100,000 shells.

## MOLLUSCA

Mollusca comes from the Latin meaning "soft bodied". Every dead shell found upon a beach is a house which was once inhabited by a living soft bodied creature. Most shells are molluscs, but not all molluscs have shells. Characteristics which all molluscs share, however, at some stages in their lives are:

**A MANTLE** - Not only does a mantle protect the organs of a shell's body with an outer layer of tissue, but also it secretes a limestone substance from its edge. This substance creates shells and later repairs the inevitable wear and tear of cracks and chips.

**A FOOT** - which allows the animal to move during at least one phase of his growth.

A simple **NERVOUS SYSTEM**

**CIRCULATORY, DIGESTIVE AND REPRODUCTIVE SYSTEMS**

Some kind of **RESPIRATION SYSTEM**

**A RADULA** or rasping organ in the mouth. S. Peter Dance on p.10 of his *Shells and Shell Collecting* describes a radula as being a tough ribbon set with rows of teeth. I don't like radulae. Something tells me Death by Radula is no joke. Bivalves don't have them, bivalves meaning those pairs of shells somehow hooked together in their middles.

## CLASSES OF MOLLUSCS

## GASTROPODA

The Phylum Mollusca is divided into seven classes and may eventually have eight. There are perhaps 70,000-80,000 one-shelled or univalve creatures called Gastropoda. Snails, whelks, conchs, and periwinkles belong to this class; all have

## The Major Groups of Living Mullusks

Figure 1. The phylum Mollusca is divided into seven classes repre-sented by the soft-bodied animals exhibiting widely differing degrees of adaptive specialization for aquatic and terrestrial life.

**I. Class Aplacophora**
Solenogasters are wormlike marine mollusks lacking a shell but with the exterior body cov-ered with shelly spicules.

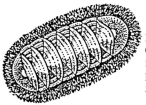

**II. Class Polyplacophora**
Chitons are limpetlike marine mollusks with eight overlapping shelly plates joined to each other by a fleshy girdle.

**III. Class Monoplacophora**
Gastroverms are cap-shaped marine mollusks with internal organs and gills paired and arranged in separate groupings.

**IV. Class Gastropoda**
Snails or univalves are marine, fresh-water, or land inhabitants, commonly with a coiled, single shell, or rarely shell-less

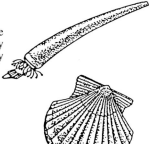

**V. Class Scaphoda**
Tusk or tooth shells are marine dwellers with curved, tubular shells open at both ends.

**VI. Class Bivalvia (Peleycypoda)**
Bivalves - the clams, oysters, and scallops- are marine and fresh-water mollusks with two valves joined by a hinge, a horny ligament and one or two muscles.

**VII. Class Cephalopoda**
The exclusively marine squids, octopuses, and nautilus are mollusks with the head region provided with tentacles, large eyes, and powerful jaws. Shell is commonly lacking or in-ternal, rarely external.

# *SEASHELLS OF THE WORLD*

## Golden Nature Guide
### Author: R. Tucker Abbott
### Illustrator: George G. Sandström

## The Anatomy of Gastropods (Univalves)

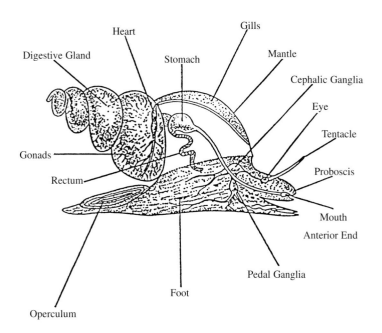

Figure 4. The Gastropods have a single shell, which is here removed to expose the gross internal anatomy. Most gastropods are shelled and have a well developed head with paired eyes and tentacles and a large foot adapted for crawling. Feeding is aided by a chitinous radula in the mouth. The mantle secretes the shell and may produce an operculum.

## The Anatomy of Bivalves (Pelecypods)

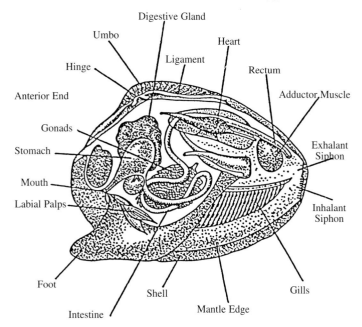

Figure 5. The bivalves–including oysters, scallops, and clams–have two shelly valves, hinged at the top, and commonly possess a hatchet-like foot adapted for burrowing. A head and raduloa are lacking; feeding is aided by the gills. The mantle is modified posteriorly into tubular siphons which draw and expel water from the mantle cavity.

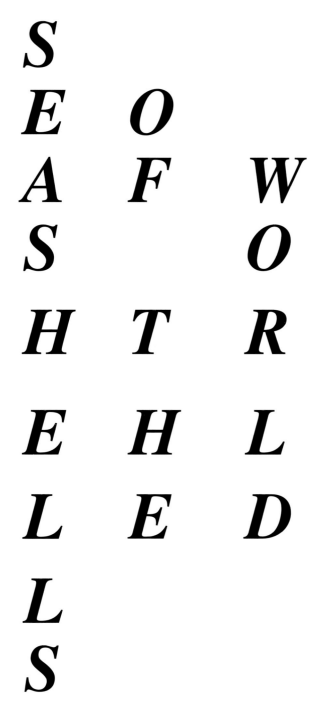

SEASHELLS
OF THE
WORLD

**Golden Nature Guide**
**Author: R. Tucker Abbott**
**Illustrator: George F. Sandström**

-44-

heads and radulae with which to shred food. Some molluscs have eyes. Like the Queen Conch some feed on grass, or like the True Tulip some are voracious predators. Most have a foot which is highly developed and well suited for crawling. Sometimes, an operculum, a brown horny structure, is attached to the end of this foot so that the animal, when disturbed or frightened, can close his front door "snap" in the hopes that marauding strangers will soon disappear.

## BIVALVIA

There are maybe 16,000-20,000 two-shelled or bivalve creatures called <u>Bivalvia</u>. Clams, oysters, scallops, and cockles all have a strong, stretching kind of an elastic ligament which keeps the two shells ajar. Scientists call these two shells valves, and the large muscles which pull them together adductor muscles. If you pick up a round ball of a cockle, and if you insert your fingernail into its crack but with gentle pressure cannot cause its two shells or valves to open - forget it. It's alive. Put him back. If he opens in a flash part way and stays open, motionless, the mollusc is dead, and by looking inside you can see poor, drooping, brown, squishy parts which must be muscle or ligament, or one or the other - anyway, they are not working any longer - so you can scrape these out and keep his often breath-taking shell.

Bivalves have no heads, but some do have eyes. They are able to feed by sucking up microscopic plant or animal matter through a siphon.

## CEPHALOPODA

The 700-1,200 living squids, nautiluses, and octopuses which make up the class <u>Cephalopoda</u> move swiftly, see keenly, and their heads are armed with "sharp, parrot-like beaks", surrounded by long flexible tentacles studded with "sucking disks". Cephalopoda have great speed, strength, and alertness. They have wonderful eyes and are predatory carnivores. They propel themselves by squirting water, and some say that squids can travel thirty miles per hour. Cephalopoda include 10,000 fossil species. I do not collect live Cephalopoda, but to see even one underwater, just once, is an unforgettable, fascinating, thrilling experience.

## AMPHINEURA

The 1,300 chitons called <u>Amphineura</u> are the elongate, primitive, flattened molluscs whose shells of eight single overlapping plates are bound together into a kind of armour by a "tough, leathery girdle", (p.23 *Shells and Shell Collecting* by S. Peter Dance). Perfect dead ones are easily found, particularly after storms. Living ones, clinging to wave crashed rocks, are another matter. If they hear you coming their own brand of super glue, (which is actually a kind of super suction), always proves superior to man's.

## SCAPHOPODA

The 1,100 Tusk shells making up the class of <u>Scaphopoda</u> consist of "tusk-like", open ended tubes lacking heads or eyes, (p.23 *Shells and Shell Collecting* by S. Peter Dance). I have never even seen one, although they are said to be common on many beaches.

## MONOPLACOPHORA

The sixth class was not really founded until 1957 when a certain mollusc considered to be a fossil was reported as having been found alive off the coast of Guatemala in 1952. Now <u>Monoplacophora</u> are a rare, deep sea, primitive group with segmented soft parts. Of the ten molluscs which belong to this class, four are extinct, and as far as I know none have ever been found anywhere near Exuma beaches.

## SUBDIVISION OF CLASSES

Unfortunately - I say unfortunately because it is so difficult to remember - the seven classes are subdivided as follows:

1. Kingdom
2. Phylum
3. Class
4. Order
5. Family
6. Genus
7. Species

Fortunately, when Linnaeus invented his Binomial System of Nomenclature, he decided that Latin would lend universality to all shell groups. Latin meant that for the first time peoples all over the world, no matter what their mother tongue, could at last recognize what each was saying to the other when it came to discussing <u>names</u> of shells.

"Oh gosh, look at what's under this seaweed. A Sunshell. It's all orange and white. Isn't it gorgeous?"

"That's not a Sunshell. That's a Butterfly Shell."

"No it's not. My mother says it's a Sunrise Tellin and she knows everything."

No fights, no tears, no fisticuffs you three children. Just move on to Linnaeus. He called it a Tellina radiata Linné 1758.

When I find a shell with which I am unfamiliar, I look it up in my favourite shell book. If the shell is particularly attractive, I try to remember its common name. Even when common names in one book differ from common names in another book, they are at least in English, and therefore easier for my kind of brain to remember than Latin names. Latin names, however, sometimes fool you. Sometimes they are singing song names. That's when I want to learn them.

Cyphoma gibbosa
Janthina janthina
Spirula spirula
Laevicardium laevigatum

you can say them a hundred times a day, or write them twice in one chapter. They still retain a peculiarly uplifting magic. Ten a year added to my list - that's my goal. Then, as I walk along a beach, I make up stories about meeting famous scientists coming from the other direction. Innocently I remark, "Oh I see you have found a Strombus gigas Linné 1758." The head scientist, who is tall and handsome, stops dead in his tracks, amazed, and says to himself, "What a remarkably learned lady." Naturally, being intrigued with such unexpected erudition, he sits himself down upon the sand and answers all my hundreds of questions concerning shells which, (so far), I have been unable to answer for myself by reading books.

I have never picked up a shell, and stood before an astounded group of admirers, intoning, "This particular shell is of this class, this order, this superfamily, this family, this genus, and this species. Amen." Instead, I feel strong admiration for those beginners who are able to give each shell two Latin names. From the lifetime of Linnaeus until today, all molluscs bear two Latin names. Linnaeus' idea was to reduce confusion, and reduce confusion he did.

When I found my first Reticulated Cowrie Helmet, Dr. R. Tucker Abbott in his *Seashells of North America*, p.116 called it just that - a Reticulated Cowrie Helmet. But when I looked up my new find in *Field Guide to Shells* by Percy Morris edited by Clench on p.181, he told me that my new shell was a Baby Bonnet. At least they both agreed that Linné had named it Cypraecassis testiculus Linné.

One scientist called my Wide Mouth Purpura, (photographed above), a Wide Mouth Purpura, and another called it a Wide Mouth Rock Shell. I try to remember Purpura patula Linné as a peaceful compromise. I happen to like the name Rooster-tail Conch, but others insist on Cock Stromb. All are satisfied with Strombus gallus Linné. As for my favourite marginella, the only reason I call it a Roosevelt's Marginella is because I learned that name before finding out that someone else called it an Orange Marginella. I have not yet memorized the Latin name everyone uses - Prunum carneum Storer.

# CHAPTER V

# WHAT TO BRING

# WHAT TO WEAR

Once upon a time, I lived in a sailboat for two years with three children and one husband. Slowly, we sailed around the world. It was interesting because when you live in North America you see things one way, and when you have finished sailing around the world for two years, you see things another way. You are no longer the same person.

In those days, there were about 30 million Indonesians, 44 million Filipinos, and 16 million Singhalese. Most of the people we met were poor. If you think about it, it is not a good idea to wear trousers if you are poor.

"How come Mummy?"

"Every time you get bigger, you need another pair. Trousers are expensive. If you only have $100 a year income, trousers are out."

"Well I'm not wearing a skirt - you can bet your life."

"It's not a skirt, Alastair. Look. It's a tube of cloth. You just fold it down when it's too long. See? You tie it like this. I'll show you."

Marongs, Sarongs, Barongs, Cloth and Jacket, men and women in that part of the world, all conform to the same clothing principle. A piece of cloth sewed into a tube wrapped around the body becomes expandable and contractible. Lengthen it? Drop it 6". Shorten it? Fold it down 6". In other Pacific islands, we met the Lava Lava and the Pareo, one long and one short, both without seams. They resembled small bed sheets instead of tubes, easy to wrap around and tuck in the waist or breast of male or female.

"It's the same idea in India, Mummy. That's where they have saris. Saris are just seven yards of cloth wrapped around you. You gave each of us one for Christmas. Remember?"

"But the tops, Fiona. You have to change the tops."

"Still, that's not much cloth. One yard maybe. If we lived in India, Grandma would buy a sari. Then when Grandma died you would get Grandma's sari. Then when you died I would get your sari. See?"

"Let's only wear Pareos and Sarongs, Mummy - let's."

"For two whole years, Mara?"

"Yes."

"Why?"

"Well this lady told me that Chiefs never invite white women to their feasts and maneabas."

"How come?"

"Because white ladies show their knees.  Chiefs don't like ladies' knees.  It's indecent.  But if you want to be naked up top, that's okay with them Mummy.  They'll invite you every time.  Fat ladies are favourites with Chiefs, Mummy.  You'll go over big."

The children laughed.

"Okay, let's wear sarongs.  It will be an adventure."

And so our family were cool in 100°F weather.  We were invited to every feast going in the Marquesas, the Tuamotus, the Tokelau, the Ellis, and we learned a lot.

We learned that bathing suits are better for swimming than are sarongs, but that for walking on beaches sarongs are a great improvement over trousers.  Sarongs made of thinnest Chinese Poplin.  For ladies, in the long ago, $10 St. Laurent see through tablecloths were great to wrap around ladies' bathing suits.  Waist to ankle is all that matters.  When you want to be sunburned, you wear your bathing suit.  When you want to be protected, you wear an ankle length pareo on top of your bathing suit.  Thinnest butterfly cotton is dry after hanging over a bush for ten minutes.  Wet trousers, after hanging over a bush for ten minutes, are clammy shark skin sandpapering your sunburned legs.  It takes hours, maybe days, for wind and sun to dry soggy blue jeans in the Exumas.  Blue jeans on Exuma beaches are a horrible hindrance.


### IDEAS OF WHAT TO BRING IN YOUR LITTLE BOAT FOR A DAY'S ADVENTURING - NECESSITIES

Something to Drink - Water is a good choice.

Two Bathing suits - one to wear and one to change into after you become wet and cold.

One Long-sleeved Shirt - the lightest, softest, fastest drying cotton you can find.  Sea Island Cotton feels delicious and seems to last forever.

One Sarong for men or One Pareo, ankle length, for women.  (The dictionary spells Pareo Pareu but in the South Seas they pronounce it Pareo.)

One Hat with a broad brim.

One Pair of Sunglasses.

One Cockle Catcher - for the home-made variety see photograph p.48 and see description p.70.

Two Beach Towels.

Suntan Creams of different strengths.

One total block Sunproof Cream for noses and lips.

One Diving Mask.

One Water Glass, or glass bottomed bucket, or water bucket, the name varying in different parts of the Bahamas (For the shape of it see upper right p.48.)

One See-Through Plastic Container with a screw or snap on lid for storing shells.

One Styrofoam Cup inside this container for baby shells.

One Straw Basket and one heavy duty garbage bag to wrap around it for keeping out the rain or spray. (If you don't have a straw basket, a brightly coloured plastic bucket will be highly visible and do just as well.)

Some Paper Napkins or a roll of Paper Towels in your picnic box to deal with Tar on your feet. Once you have patted dry your feet, liberal applications of suntan cream before rubbing and scrubbing work miracles. So do old beach sticks if the tar is very thick.

Don't play this special game unless first of all you invent your own container for shells. If you begin to like this game, you will feel desperate at the inadvertent smashing of your treasures.

I once read about little plastic vials for teeny shells. I used to dismiss teeny shells with an airy wave of my uncaring hand, but my husband taught me to be passionate about them. It was all a matter of how best to display their charms, emphasizing their size rather than feeling diminished by their insignificance.

The trouble with little plastic vials is they always get lost. I don't lose them. They lose themselves. I'm always in a hurry. The children are always screaming and yelling, "Come on Mummy. What are you doing?" Meanwhile where are yesterday's little plastic vials?

An acceptable alternative to these elusive vials is a clear plastic soup or pasta shell container. Mine is about ten inches high and has a brilliant orange screw-on top. It is hard to lose something so big and colourful. Into this I put a styrofoam cup. If I find big shells, they fit into my big container. If I find little shells, they fit into my styrofoam cup. Once this styrofoam cup is safely inside the plastic container, it cannot tip over. If I find too many shells, there is a place in my water bucket or my diving mask for them. But this excessive bounty always makes me nervous. If I don't hold the water bucket or the diving goggles in my lap all during what is usually a sloshy and bouncy journey homewards, someone invariably steps on my finds, leaving crunched up ruin instead of irreplaceable beauty. This is **NOT** a good way to end the day. The person who broke your first True Tulip will hurt; you will hurt; and this hurt is avoidable.

**OPTIONAL**

Footwear - see Chapter X - People on our boat prefer divers' booties.

Meat Tenderizer - I wish I could remember to bring it for those ubiquitous Sting Rays I have yet to see slash someone.

A Candle and some Matches - After you have stepped onto a black Sea Egg or Sea Urchin stumble back to shore. Pat the place dry. Light a candle. Drip the hot wax directly onto the broken-off black needles sticking out of your skin, and be glad you remembered your candle and matches. The pain will soon become bearable. Do NOTHING ELSE. In a few days or a few weeks, the needles will disappear. Meanwhile they will not hurt.

Camera.

Something to Eat.

## CAMERA

If you take a camera to the beach, here are some tips from a beginner.

My daughter Mara, aged 13, was an incredible photographer - even if, in her Mother's opinion, this was mostly due to osmosis. Meanwhile her Mother languished in despair, read every photography book for beginners on the market, and continuously threw away 100 out of 100 slides. One day Mara said to her in a quizzical voice,

> "How much did that lens cost you Mummy?"

> "Oh I don't know - about $200 maybe."

In an identical tone she continued,

> "How much did that filter cost you Mummy?"

> "Oh about $1."

> "You haven't graduated to special effects yet Mummy, so how come you always use a filter? Do you mind me asking? Why?"

I didn't mind her asking why, and that was a very interesting question. Now I never use filters for Filtering except on Special Effect days. I use them for Protection, and each of my lenses has a filter screwed on to its top. In my opinion lens caps were not made for the trade winds or salt air of the Bahamas in winter, especially during storms. The minute I see a picture I need to take, I unscrew my filter, put it in the top of my bathing suit, take the picture, and then screw the filter back on to the camera. This habit has saved my lenses a lot of grief.

About going to sea with my camera in a little open boat? I hate it. But by wrapping my camera in a thin cotton scarf which I then enclose in the thickest available beach towel I mitigate some of the potential hazards. Beach towel, cotton scarf and camera go plunk into a brilliant coloured bucket with a bright, excessively clean Conch shell on top to remind people, "That's Mummy's camera". My camera is the only camera which usually survives each winter.

If on extremely rough days I am tempted to take my camera to the beach, a temptation I always regret, I put the bucket into a heavy duty garbage bag and tie a knot. The second I reach the beach, I remove the garbage bag. As for changing film or lenses on an Exuma beach, my succinct advice is "Don't".

## IDEAS FOR PACKING
Heavy duty garbage bags hold about six folded towels apiece.

Clothes fit neatly into straw baskets. Straw baskets stay dry inside of knotted heavy duty garbage bags. Plastic buckets are great for everything:

> Lunches
> Rubbish
> Empty nasty tins
> Other people's beach litter
> Cameras

Brightly coloured plastic buckets cheer everyone. I spend a lot of time shopping for plastic buckets before each year's vacation. They are probably the most important item on my list. In the wilderness Beauty matters. The more you use and depend on something, the more beautiful it should be. Plastic buckets with chrome handles are disastrous if your visit lasts longer than two weeks. Chrome rusts. Plastic stays serviceable for years.

## ADVICE TO PEOPLE WHO DETEST SAND OR TAR ON THEIR CRUISING BOATS OR IN THEIR BEDS
Please don't read the following if sand scattered everywhere makes you feel cozy. Please don't read the following if you have a dog on board. Dogs make all of this information irrelevant.

Train your children and your guests from Day One. No footwear of any kind whatsoever is allowed into your little boat. It may be removed and rinsed. It may be stored in a tarry bucket. It may **NOT** be worn. This is because footwear, no matter how careful the wearer, often picks up tar. Tar transferred from one boat to the other causes a proud owner's heart to burn with outrage.

Every single item going from the beach into the little boat must be rinsed on its bottom, (like a plastic bucket) or banged, (like a straw basket) or shaken first, (like a beach towel).

All limbs which enter the boat must be free of sand or else plunged into the ocean.

All feet must be inspected for TAR before entering the boat.

All these rules may sound laborious. If you are ADAMANT about them, each evening becomes a game with a good deal of laughter attendant to departure from the beach. Three year olds can rub Auntie's foot, and five year olds **LIKE** taking tar off with sticks. It's interesting. Children adore catching out Mummy or Daddy with patches of sand still sticking to the backs of their legs. They are eager to help you remove it, usually with devilish ingenuity. Your house is your kingdom. So is your boat. Guests laugh and say, "Oh she's crazy", but I notice they come back again next year.

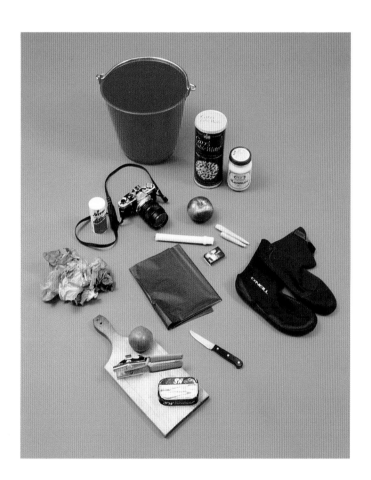

# OPTIONAL

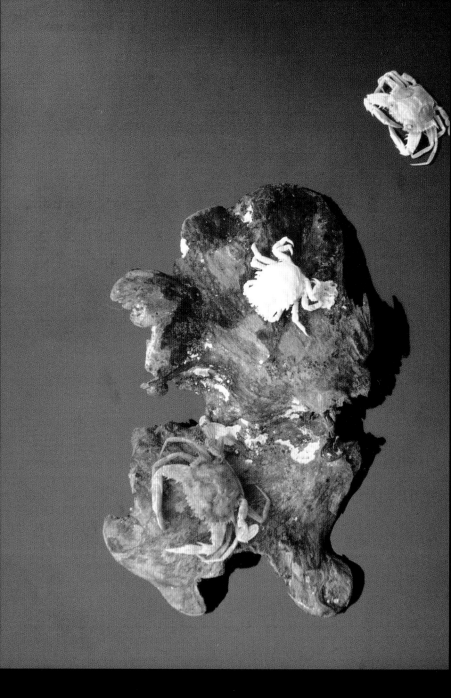

# CHAPTER VI

# WHAT ELSE
# TO COLLECT

Shells are enhanced by the beauties which surround them. Sea fans, corals, jeweled reef fishes all add to the lustre of each perfect find.

If you are not a scientist or a serious collector, but have become enamoured with your arrangements of **IMPERMANENT ART**, (see p.123), you will find that objects from the shells' natural surroundings add charm to each of your displays.

## CORAL

Fascinating varieties of coral wash up on beaches. During and after storms, one of my eyes is always busy looking for shells, while the other is busy looking for coral. I almost never see a whole piece of coral. Usually I see some little tip or sprig of something quite white, sometimes thick and bulbous, sometimes thin and lacy, sticking up from its hiding place in seaweed or sand.

If seaweed is my problem, I try to turn my fingers into spiders' feet, lightly lightly prying off the glued on pieces, rinsing them in the ocean, then peeling off more pieces, always in layers - layer by slow layer.

If sponges are attached, (and the sponges are usually ugly), I take even greater care.

If my problem turns into hills and valleys of sand, swirls left behind by raging seas, I softly dig trenches in and around my prize hoping against hope a new and entrancing shape will soon emerge.

It is easy, after miles and miles of empty trudging, to suddenly spy a perfect piece of coral and become so excited that you yank it from the sand. With happy anticipation, you jerk away its offensive clinging sponges. If, however, your eagerness leaves your hands filled with broken fragments of lacy fronds, you will feel dismay. Glue is not the same as Nature. Break your coral, and then, when you gaze at your Treasure Tray, all you will see is **GLUE**. No cool undersea kingdoms, teeming with jewel fish will beguile your mind. Mournful "why's", reproachful "if only's" will boomerang around instead. The idea of Impermanent Art is to create a perfect feeling. Glue gets in the way of perfection.

In addition to lacy sprays of coral, calcified baby trees of coral, thick, bulbous underwater flowers of coral, whole areas of ocean inside mangrove flats seem carpeted with spiny, woven needles of coral. There, so much of it washes ashore, the only question to trouble any collector is "Which?"

## CRABBIES

In order for crabbies to be realistic, they must have all their little claws plus their two eyes. When I am wading in knee deep water I often see a perfect dead crabbie floating by. Sometimes he hasn't even died; he has just abandoned his smaller shell in anticipation of growing a larger one. If guests realize you treasure crabbies, they think it is great fun to seek them out. Grown-ups as well as children find this game excessively amusing, especially when they realize that you have very high standards. You accept nothing less than perfect crabbies.

There are many fascinating varieties of crabbies. The ochre yellow crab with black-tipped claws is very small. A two inch white crab duplicates in miniature its larger restaurant cousin. Undoubtedly the cousin is more tasty. A prehistoric bulgy type has spindly legs seemingly miles too long for his odd, puffed-up body. Often we find red crabs, or blue crabs, or the kind of crab which stores food on the end of his nose. Adding the Crab Game to your Shell Game brings new dimensions to each.

**SEA FANS**

Unless you are the sort of person who hammers beautiful large fans to your walls for display, it is more rewarding to concentrate on smaller sizes for your Impermanent Art displays. Shape and colour determine my choices. Bright yellow and bright purple are my favourites; purple turning blue and yellow turning pink - two toned fans are my second favourites. Shellers take your choice on days during or after a storm, when hundreds of dead ones are washed up on beaches or rocks in certain well defined territories, because fans torn living from ocean floors are not allowed in this Shell Game.

Shape is important. Without an intriguingly artistic or beautiful shape, fans don't add much to your collection. Plain fans do not make a viewer think of water-glass oceans populated by undulating gardens. Part of the pleasure of collecting for Impermanent Art is your audience's gasp of surprise when he surveys your dazzling arrangement. If you are lucky in your beach journey, you might also find

a little rock cast ashore, and growing from this little rock a sprightly purple feather sea fan.

A nice thing about sea fans is they fade very slowly and may be used again year after year. They don't quaver the heartstrings with mournful disappointment as do Conchs or Sunrise Tellins, (whose colours diminish month by month with relentless obduracy).

## SPONGES AND BOTTOMS OF SEA FANS

Sea fan bottoms which have parted from their hosts and floated in the ocean for hours and days, turn into highly polished, very small wood carvings of entrancing shape. Their muted colour becomes an excellent foil to brilliant shells and a perfect home for certain types of crabbies.

It is hard to find a pretty sponge. Most of them seem to be wiry sausages of repulsive character, but every once in awhile an unusual shape and perfect size greets the eye.

## SPONDYLUS, (pp.87, 152)

A half a spondylus with a stunning orange back, nice sharp spines, and an inner shell rimmed with the same colour . . . Mmmmmmmmm . . .

> "But I don't collect shells unless they're **PERFECT**. He's missing his other half."

That's true, but the thing about big halves of Spondyli or Tiger Lucinas, (p.61), in perfect condition is that they make fine and devoted mothers for guarding babies. Who wants a lot of babies anyway? They're so small you cannot see them. Any wind blows them all across your arrangements. They're a vexing nuisance. . . . until you arrange them in their mother shell. Now prepare for oohs and aahs of applause. Your troubles are ended.

Tiniest Tulips, glossy Rice Shells, your newest Spiny Cockle Baby, a glamorous yellow Pecten, a Sea Biscuit too impossible to start off life so unprepared and defenceless, baby Limpets and Nerites and Tegulas discussing their home which was, crowding close to junior Mossy Arks, Worm Shells boisterously worming their way into other children's conversations. With all these infants safely ensconced upon the bosom of an orange Spondylus or a pink rimmed Tiger Lucina, beauty adorns your day, and baby-sitting is a chore of the past.

## FOSSILIZED SHELLS

Some people avoid the fossilized. But fossils give a feeling of Permanence to Impermanent Art, (p.123). Such is life - a mixture: the crowing of clamorous babies amidst the laughter of more maturely rounded beauties. Neither babies nor adults are perfect without the foil of some venerable sage. I call my favourite fossil Confucius with his beard, guarding the morals, nurturing the motivations of all my too many, gadabout butterfly children. These infants Need conversation with the Wisdom of the Ages. They Need, on a daily basis, what is missing from so many nuclear families - a Grandpa. That is why my fossilized Angular Triton plays so important a role. It is he who is saying,

"Now children part of the Now is the Future. How will you like your face 20 years from today? Discipline, my children. Life is not all singing, nor all these newly captivating colours of dress. The Serious and the Grave are important too. Come. Concentrate."

**PORTUGUESE FLOATS**

A Portuguese Float Day is a day for singing Songs in the Wilderness Day. It is a day of excitement for all. Who will find palest lavender? Who will find silvery blue tinged from years of travel across the high seas? Perhaps deepest bottle green will win the day. Some explorers prefer miniatures, some like their floats encased in romantic woven string. Whatever a sheller's preference, finding a glass float, just one brilliantly colored glass ball floated free from some far away fisherman's nets, is worth all those weary steps inspecting fraudulent bottles deliberately buried where sand is the deepest and tar the blackest.

**A CONCH WITH CORAL GROWING FROM HIS BACK**
I have a conch so old he has no lip.  Upon his hoary shell grows a tree of white coral.  "Age can be remarkable and beautiful," he is reassuring to all who think with distaste of rickety bones and aching backs hitched to protruding bellies.

"I am the example of what you can become.  Just a little practice every day my darlings, and Age need hold no terrors."

# CHAPTER VII

# WHERE

# WHAT

# WHEN

# WHERE

## THE "TERRITORIAL IMPERATIVE"

This Shell Game is a guessing game - a game of outwitting the shell. With this tide, on this day, in this wind, where is a perfect specimen likely to be hiding?

No matter how many rules I make for myself, unexpected, dumbfounding and frustrating exceptions break them all the time.

Robert Ardrey wrote a book called *The Territorial Imperative*. I agree. Certain shells, in the Exumas have territories - strictly defined, quite small areas of beach and water where they **ALWAYS** lie. The trick is to find the exact area. Then you can return to it, year after year, until a storm completely alters its appearance, and you have to start all over again. (Fortunately such an extremely major storm seldom happens.) Once you find your area, every day something new will be waiting in that exact spot. It may not be collectable because it doesn't match your standards, but every fifth or sixth day, almost certainly, you will be able to pounce upon one or two perfect specimens.

This year one of my places measures three feet by two feet. It is only an elongated pool which appears on a particular bend of a particular sandbank at lowest low tide. The 15 speckled Tellins I have collected there over a two week period would make any king jealous: Tiny ones, enormous ones, all of them perfect - all of them having different, fragile, and rare colourings. Who eats Tellins for Tea? If I shoveled under a sand hill, would I find Somebody Shelly munching away?

What you have to do is THINK. Where is this dumb shell you absolutely have to have? Where is his home? Why? Learned Tomes tell you anything you want to know about Live Shells, and nothing at all about Dead Shells. So you need to become your own Learned Tome.
Who eats who? When? At night? During storms? At Low Tide? Where?

When I see an enormous live King Helmet on a sandbank, looking like a tiny, triangular, stick up mountain, I can't resist picking him up. I want to know exactly how beautiful he is. Often he will be slurping brilliant green poison all over a tightly clutched sand dollar – slurp, slurp, slurp. So now you know whenever you see hundreds of dead sand dollars, there ought to be live Helmet Hunters about. Couldn't one of them have just caught the flu and died recently - unchipped and perfect - awaiting your eager shouts of joy? Just one? If an octopus eats all kinds of things does he sometimes leave, outside of his hole, perfect empty shells waiting for your next eager visit? If an immense True Tulip lives in a tiny pond near the Low Tide Sand Bar that you sometimes visit, isn't his pond worth an occasional investigation? Even when he doesn't care to share his luncheon with me, I love staring at his marvelous peregrinations, his inky black body, and I try not to fantasize what a twelve inch long shell would do for my collection.

## OUTSIDE BEACHES

are beaches which edge islands along their Deep Ocean side. Some Outside Beaches have no shells whatsoever. You can walk for miles. Year after year of walking brings you zero.

Other Outside Beaches will always have something. Usually during or after storms you will find Sea Biscuits, or Sea Eggs, or Sunshells, or dried baby Starfish, or marvelous branches of Coral, or Tritons. Sometimes even a Measled Cowrie becomes Prize of the Day.

If you are the kind of traveller who comes back year after year, and if you become passionately attached to this Shell Game, your mental notes will make you veer away from miles of empty exhaustion, and head you straight towards those beaches with which you are familiar, and from which the unexpected may occur at any moment. Experience will be your teacher.

## INSIDE BEACHES

or beaches which face calmer, interior oceans, seem to be the worst, stupidest, yuckiest, most non-yielding, sand-fly infested beaches that have ever existed, until you make yourself think of TERRITORY.

If, in the eye of your mind, you can imagine the word TERRITORY day-glowed orange, in foot high capitals, then Inside Beaches are <u>much</u> easier to work than Outside Beaches, and <u>much</u> more productive. If you are familiar with them, you will remember the exact spot to zoom for, and the exact spot is almost never more than 100 feet by 100 feet. If you are unfamiliar with them, all the more fun perfecting your new role of Hunter and Explorer.

## STOMACHS

Some shell books suggest that stomachs of fish or Starfish contain exciting finds. So the next time you catch a Grouper or a Jewfish, you might see if these shell books are right. I would feel sad killing a Starfish.

## SCUBA DIVING

Michael Humfrey on p.305 of his fascinating *Sea Shells of the West Indies* describes a kind of ooze which surrounds the bases of some reefs. Into this ooze drop dead shells which remain in lovely condition due to the soft protection around them. In Jamaica, in 1966, some enterprising scuba divers fashioned wire mesh cylindrical sieves. Diving to about 60 feet, he says they scooped up handfuls of ooze and debris, which, when sieved through their cylinders yielded choice, shining species - prime reward for such hard work.

## ROCKY ISLETS

Once in a great while - other people - not I - have found something stunning where it seems impossible for anything to withstand the high tide pounding and crashing of continuous surf. The trouble with small islands made only of rock is that they lack trees and sand. Without anchorage of this kind, you need a good boatman who shouts, "Jump", as he darts in on one wave, and a brave sheller willing to instantly obey, before his boat is swamped by the next.

# WHAT

## SHAPES AND COLOURS

Never look for a perfect shell lying on top of the sand awaiting your gasp of pleasure.  Your dreams will be doomed to lacerations of disappointment.  Everyone will say, "Oh goodie, look what I found".  They will have Treasures for Treasure Trays.  You will have paper plates of rinsed out Throw Aways.

Unless you are unbelievably lucky, you will almost never find a shiny, perfect shell, nicely placed, right side up, fully out of the sand expecting your surprise pounce.  It happens.  But in the Exumas seldom.

Look for **SHAPES**.  Memorize the shape of the shell you are ardent to possess.  When you peer through the surface of the sea don't look for a shell, look for its shape.  The shape you are looking for is often covered with fine gray mud, and it looks like a rock - except - has anyone ever seen a butterfly rock?  Walking into the sun,  investigate the tiniest gleams and winks of light on any sand flat, because they may be mirror reflections from only one piece of your shell.  A streak of orange, a too shiny touch of white, a wet gleam of pink - these are **COLOURS** to investigate.  When you think a piece of what you have found belongs to a whole shell, start digging very tenderly, because if you pull vigorously at the tip of a Sunshell, you may find, too late, that you have broken it in half.

That's all you need for your first day of this Shell Game - a determination to investigate suspicious looking rocks, a refusal to believe that that sudden glare of sun came from some buried bottle, and a knowledge that he who says wearily, "Oh that's just a piece of old yellow paper plate - I wish boats burnt their garbage", is a sucker for missing the best Find of the Day.

## OLD SHELLS LEADING TO NEW

One of my tricky tricks is noticing patches of beach covered with beat up shells which all come from the same family.  For instance, on one beach, on one island, you may always find weathered, uncollectable Wide Mouth Purpuras.  On another beach there may be some remnants of a cracked in half Atlantic Gray Cowrie or even a Measled Cowrie.  Certain shells seem to live on certain beaches in certain places.  One never ever seems to find them anywhere else except after a Major Storm.  (Major Storms change all the rules.)  Year after year I return to my favourite Measled Cowrie beach with my heart beating fast.  I reason that if I continually notice the worn out husks of what I am seeking around my feet, maybe this year, this visit I will finally be lucky.  Maybe I will find a Perfect Atlantic Gray Cowrie, shiny as if just made, or a Wide Mouth Purpura without any horrid holes in its back.  When patience, persistence and reasoning pays off, I can crow "Look, look - I finally found it - I was right", and feel elated for weeks afterwards.

# WHEN

## STORMS

The bigger the storm the better.  In some places, the time to look is just as the storm commences.  As the first ominous surge begins to grow, letting yourself be rocked and rattled by monster waves seems hopeless, especially if the water is roiled gray, and devoid of clarity. But, standing in waist deep water, either with a water-glass or a mask, sometimes you can see colour being whirled around through all that gray. Grab at the colour quickly and lightly. This is the way I found my rarest, perfect Rough American Scallop, (p.64).

During the storm itself, you must become an Adventurer. Even if the wind is howling so strongly it will blow you flat, or sand-blast you to death with stinging sand, still, strange things happen during storms - miracle things. They don't wait. They're only there from tide to tide. Undoubtedly they will be swallowed up, washed away, or pulverized by the next incoming rage of wave.

After the storm has finished, and the ocean is exhausted innocence exclaiming, "Who me - I'm as calm as a baby - I wouldn't hurt anyone", that's the funnest time of all. Anything, anything can happen after a storm. All bets are off for a few days. All carefully garnered knowledge is out the window. Surprises are Kings at any bend of any beach.

## FLAT CALMS

On rarest days in the Exumas the ocean is so extraordinarily calm that peering through 20 feet of water is as clear as if all those myriad fishes were swimming around inside your cocktail glass. You can see **EVERYTHING**. All the secrets of the seas are yours. Sometimes for an hour. Sometimes for 12. You stand dizzy with disbelief, and unbelieving. **QUICK**. Stop everything. Get moving. Find a good driver to drive the boat. Stand up in the bow. Maybe you can hold on to a bow rope, maybe you can balance. Bring a water bucket. Look for **COLOUR**; look for **SHAPE**; don't look for shells. Yell at the boat to stop when you see a flash of orange or yellow. Jump in if it is shallow, or dive in if it is deep. You'll be surprised. Three or four feet of water is often the perfect depth. Remember the place. Soon you will have a collection of places. Be sure to save them at the back of your mind for a new inspection trip on your next Flat Calm day.

Water buckets are used when you are growing weary of jumping in and out of the water and you want to be sure of what you are investigating. If the driver is bad, and his mind wanders towards slow cruising green sharks, or eagle Sting Rays swimming with prehistoric motion, be careful. A slicing-you-up-propeller is no joke. Boats that hit rocks or beaches while standing-in-the-bow shellers hunt shells are no joke either. Six to ten year old children are the best players of this part of the Shell Game, just as two to three year olds are the best players on small beaches. Perhaps because they are so little and therefore so close to the beach they tend to make the most breathtaking finds.

If you happen upon an ocean sandbank, and it is surrounded by fairly deep water, even if there are no shells on the bank itself, wade out to sea, waist or shoulder deep. If it is mirror calm, you can cover vast areas just by wading and peering. The more adventurous explorers can swim. You are bound to hear shrieks of excitement greeting discoveries which are usually not available anywhere else.

Even when the day is not mirror calm, boats often go to beaches for picnics, and if the beach is out of the wind, sometimes there is a thin edge of calm near the shore. If you give your driver some warning and stand up, often you can see the unexpected. Some say Polaroid glasses are magic for this kind of hunting. Whenever I wear them, I feel like Dorothy donning her Green Spectacles when she visited the Land of Oz - Ordinary instantly becoming Extraordinary.

### FLAT CALMS AND A COCKLE CATCHER
"What I need Sandy is a cockle catcher."

"A cockle catcher?"

"Well, when you drive the boat, and the water feels like 30 degrees below zero, I don't want to go swimming. If I had a cockle catcher, I wouldn't need to."

"I'll make you one, darling, I will."

And so he did for Christmas Day. Now I never go shelling without it. On p.48, you can see a picture of this generous, homemade endeavour - a long hollow black tube to which my husband attached a tiny dark green, aquarium fishnet.

### LOW TIDE
Wade around. Odd sparkles and flashes of colour in strange shapes are worth bending down to investigate. In cold water bare feet can become as dexterous as arms or hands. They just need practice. A Cockle Catcher is very handy, but sometimes you are in five feet of water without one, and with no way of marking your find.

Long lines of undulating seaweed bear inspection no matter how fearsome. Floating in a few feet of water wearing a mask is fascinating, because suddenly Fearsome turns to Awesome yielding cockles as gaudy as butterflies. Some of these cockles are just dead, and their colour will make all your companions wild with jealousy.

People who don't like to dive can peer through water buckets in waist deep water. All shell books agree that Low Tide is the best time for Hunting. Sometimes, however, Low Tide is inconvenient, and any tide can bring Exceptions to any Shell Rule.

### LOW TIDE, ROUGHISH WATER, AND OLIVE OIL
When I'm really impatient with day after day of **BAD WEATHER**, and when I do not feel like swimming because the water is freezing, I'll go to a place where I know brand new shells **OUGHT** to have just died. A beach edged with a gray kind of grass where murderous Pen Shells make their homes is interesting to explore during or after certain kinds of storms.

Here is a fascinating exercise even if you find nothing. Watch the direction of the wind and pour a few caps full of olive oil into the water. (Sometimes I have collected shells for three weeks, and still have not used up even half a small bottle.)

If you try this clever idea you will be in for a fine surprise. If you are out of olive oil, safflower, peanut or sardine oil are perfectly adequate, non-polluting substitutes.

## LOW TIDES - SANDBANKS - (THE DRY KIND)

On the Inside some sandbanks live far out to sea and only appear like great white Whales during the Lowest Tides of the year. These are my happiest places for adventure. The ones I have explored were hard, not squelchy. But if you adore bare feet the way I do - be careful, be careful, be careful.

One year, I, (who knows everything there is to know about bare feet), while singing a little song and running through innocuous puddles on a wild, far-out-to-sea sandbank, cut myself so badly that fear of Gangrene kept me awake the whole following night. A white sandbank, a clear puddle, a hundred year old, completely bleached white conch, wholly buried except for its razor edge, meant three horrible gashes to my foot, with me sitting alone on the sand, 20 miles from anywhere - dazed, terrified, and stunned. As I regarded what should have been interesting white strings protruding from my foot, and as I watched brilliant blood oozing over too white sand, I vowed I would always walk, never run, on the ocean sandbanks that live far out to sea.

## LOW TIDES - SANDBANKS - (THE WET KIND)

The wet kind of sandbank in the middle of cuts or bights is so exhausting, especially for anybody with a bad leg or a bad back, that in spite of greedy desire, doubtful memory of pain may dissuade you from making all that effort. Each slurpy step sinks you down from six inches to a foot. Walking one mile of small wet sandbank equals marching three upon hard-packed beach. A handy aid in diminishing exhaustion is

## A COPY OF THE SUN, MOON AND TIDE TABLES

This is a small, thin, and excessively useful pamphlet which you can obtain by sending a little money and writing the Director of

> The Bahamas Meteorological Department
> The Climatology Section, Ground Floor, Boulevard Building
> Thompson Blvd., P.O. Box N-8330
> Nassau, N.P., Bahamas
> Telephone:    809-325-4048/9
>                      809-326-7596

Some nice characteristics about these tables are their light weight, their single pages for each month of the year, and the hours they state for the moon rising and falling. However, *The Yachtsman's Guide to the Bahamas*, which is republished every year, also lists the Tide Tables if not in so compact a form. And, although its Phases of the Moon do not include rising and setting hours, the reader may prefer all of his information located in one book.

The exact time of Low Tide on the chart depends on where you are, but even if it is out by half an hour, it is at least a helpful indication. If you go exploring at really Low Tide as opposed to half Low Tide, the sandbanks have had that much longer to drain and become hard.

# CHAPTER VIII

# CLUES TO

# COCKLES

# COCKLES

Common Egg Cockles says who?  Oh Cockles that lie beneath the blue green sea waiting to be found.  Cockles silvered by a silver moon, sung to by Ospreys.

They are not common for me.  I call Cockles "Golden Egg Cockles".  When a Golden Egg Cockle Day arrives I have to flee, I have to fly from care and machinery that whirs.  I have to embrace the soothing narcotic of Golden Egg Cockles - gems of the seas.

I am always aglow with anticipation on my Golden Egg Cockle Days.  What will I find?  Will my prize be pure white, large and smooth - some glossy fantasia of Oriental pearl?  Might it have edges echoing Amethysts from Siberia?  Sometimes faint triangles of yellow and orange repeating each other in patterns of V stun my senses.  But still - after all these years - I am slave to the Golden Egg Cockle with its yellow and orange sun glows of colour.  When I find one of these, I leap great leaps of celebration.

Finding Cockles is different from discovering Sunshells on Inside Beaches.  You might have to cover five miles of sand before you finally reach the territory where treasure troves of Sunshells lie week after week.

Not so with Cockles.  Choose any old Inside Beach.  Walk along the shore until you come to bunches of broken, or perforated or worn out Cockle Shells.  Even perfect half Cockles will do.  However, these are NOT what you want.  Most Shell Game addicts prefer perfection.  But since you are a hunter playing a detective game, you are looking for clues.  These bits and fragments of Cockle are clues to whole ones, hiding nearby, rocking gently in some glassy shallows, pristine, perfect, and just dead.

Wade out into the Ocean.  At about knee depth, if it is Low Tide, you might notice some revolting black seaweed.  This is a type of sunken seaweed resting on the ocean floor.  It is horrid.  It is not crisp, fresh, wouldn't-mind-a-bed-of-it seaweed.  It is mushy, black, tarantulas-live-inside-it-seaweed.

STOP!  Take a deep breath and watch carefully as this seaweed rolls gently back and forth with the tide.

I am not brave.  I don't like tarantulas.  So usually I wait around, standing just outside the edge of all this black mass.  If I see something - flash - in goes my hand; quickly I make a grab, and, never able to control my shudder of disgust, hope against hope the creature I pick up is not alive and well.  Usually he is.  When all this becomes too gruesome for words, I fetch my water bucket from the beach, (p.48).  I am determined that my water bucket is going to eliminate all that agonizing hesitation, that pounce for the wrong shell.  The trouble with water buckets is that they are not as agile as eyes.  With eyes you just reach.  But with a water bucket, you have to float your water bucket on the surface of the sea; you have to watch your hand reaching through the ocean beneath the glass of the water bucket, in other words, you have to juggle several things at once, and sometimes while you are juggling so fast you lose your Cockle. It all boils down to choice. Cockles or Tarantulas, Cowardly Custards or Brave as Lions.

> "Don't be silly, Mummy, tarantulas don't live in seaweed. Don't you know anything? Tarantulas live on the land. Daddy tell Mummy about tarantulas. She's just the dumbest . . ."

Alastair was right. He was only three years old. He was standing right in the middle of this nightmare stuff, his little stick-like legs just waiting for tarantulas to bite.

That's when it's time to stop the scientific investigation of this type of seaweed, even if it does contain thousands of other surprises in addition to Golden Egg Cockles. That's when it is time to keep wading further on out to sea until the water is waist high or shoulder high.

Cockles which lie open and flat with their shiny sides up are easy to see under four feet of water. Their colour will immediately catch your eye. However, Cockles closed into tight little balls, Cockles upside down filled with sand, Cockles one half buried with the other half waving vertically about, even when the water is as clear as clear, are much harder to recognize. If you can learn to concentrate on the upside down shape as well as the colourful right side up shape, you may find what someone else has missed. Good Luck Shellers! On the days when Sunshells aren't around, Golden Egg Cockles are my absolute favourite shells ever.

# SUNSHELLS OR SUNRISE TELLINS OR TELLINA RADIATA

There are two types.  One has horizontal growth bands of white, sometimes pale, thin white, sometimes broad, thick white, curving lengthwise around the shell and covering solid colours such as snowdrop white or lemon yellow.  Occasionally these bands are crossed by faint rays, but more often there are no rays at all.  I have never found this shell except on Outside Beaches.

## TELLINA RADIATA - ANOTHER KIND

Another Sunshell has rays of the sun radiating outward from the hinge of its shell. In the Exumas, I usually find this example on Inside Beaches, but sometimes, especially after storms, a few will be discovered high upon Outside Beaches.

When you search for a Sunshell, don't look for the whole shell. Usually you will only see a tiny piece of it. Sometimes one half of a shell points upwards from a wide expanse of sand flat. Other times, two tips of a completely buried shell look as if they were the ears of some small rabbit hiding in some secret underground hole. Often this shell is upside down, full of sand and water. When it is, it looks completely different from the same kind of shell turned right side up. Sand is dull. Even a tiny piece of a right side up Sunshell on a sandbank against the sun will be shining. Therefore look for something shiny. It does not matter how small - the smallest fragment may be a "part of the main". When you take a walk against the sun, when the sun is shining into your eyes, its reflection upon a piece of shell will flash like a mirror. A puddle maybe? Sometimes it's a shell pretending to be a puddle. However, if the sun is at your back, you will miss all these mirror reflection clues for shells at the periphery of your vision, only finding the ones lying dead ahead of your footsteps. Therefore, **AGAINST THE SUN** is good advice to remember if Shell Hunter Extraordinaire is your aim for the day.

## HUNTING INSIDE BEACHES FOR BRILLIANT RAYED SUNSHELLS

Only search at Low Water. It's no good muttering to yourself, "But they're always here - just in this one single spot. What is the matter?"

The problem may be that you are looking during Half Tide. If this is true, you can be as diligent as you like, swim for as long you want, and wade for as many miles as you can manage, but the probability of your finding any Sunshells at all is zero. This isn't true for other shells in other places, but for Inside Beach Sunshells Dead Low Water of the day is your only answer. The colour of the water in the cuts will be a mind boggling turquoise. The sand flats on either side of the water will be dry. If even six inches of tide has already turned, sand will sweep over your beauties burying them completely until your next day's search.

If you want to find my favourite kind of Sunshell, look for a cut which not only runs between sandbanks, but also connects Inside and Outside waters. Somewhere, on one side or the other or both, there is a territory, often only two to three hundred feet in area. You will be astonished at the bounty of just-dead Sunshells in these spots. You cannot believe the colour of their shocking pink and purple rays. Viewing melted, glazed lemon drops at the centre of orange, sinking suns, makes you feel superior to any Inca guarding his treasure. These shells are here year after year? Are you the only one who knows their exact spot?

## PARTRIDGE TUN SHELLS

As with Cockles so with Partridge Tun Shells. Particularly just after storms we encounter coveys of these aptly named shells - Mummies and Daddies and Babies all crowded together. Old ones are faded and chipped. Perfect ones are richly brown with unbroken edges.

Prizes sometimes appear on the beach. At other times, if you follow the Cockle rule, in three feet or four feet of water, new Tuns - all covered with soft brown skin, perhaps with poor dead creatures still inside, may be rocking together. These dead creatures smell dreadfully. But if you bury their shells for a few days in sand, as described on p.129, you will soon solve your horrid problem.

No smell, but a shell all lovely and clean will be yours after just a few rinses in the ocean. I scrape off the dead skin with a soft stick, a toothbrush, or a fingernail. I never do any of this unless, in the beginning, my Tun is absolutely perfect without a single crack. A perfect specimen is worth all your patient labour. Your shell becomes so glowing, so shiny, and so vibrant with colour that when you place him upon your newest Sea Fan, it feels for an instant as if some charming partridge from some wild Scottish hillside had just flown in for an evening's visit.

The good news about Partridge Tun Shells is that when you are barefoot they are easier to work to the surface of the ocean than Cockles. Cockles require the best sense of balance. If you tilt even slightly towards one side or the other, the Cockle slides off the top of your foot. Not heeding your cry of dismayed frustration, he deliberately floats away from even the most frantic fingers or toes. Partridge Tuns, on the other hand, are far more accommodating. All one needs is a toe inserted into their openings for quick, easy speed of delivery.

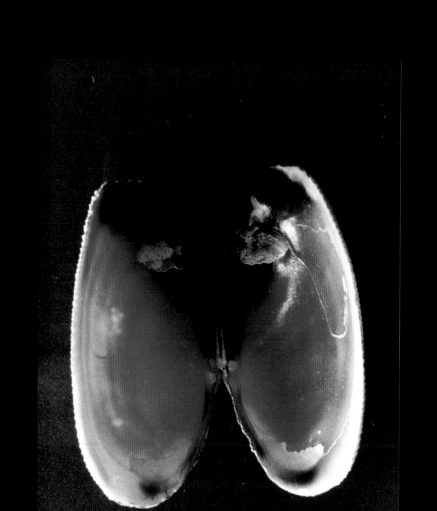

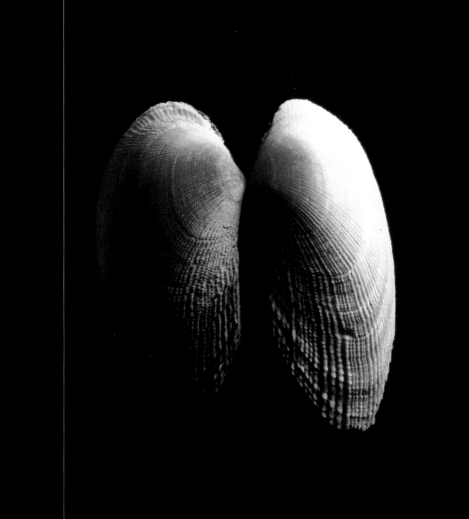

## GAUDY ASAPHIS

A fresh, newly dead Gaudy Asaphis is as breathtaking as a rose. Unfortunately, Time ruins the colours of Gaudy Asaphis just as irrevocably as it withers roses. Rayed, royal purple with indigo edges, orange as shiny as new carnelian dipped into butterscotch, yellow with purple, purple with orange - brown, yellow, and purple all mixed together - these shells are Kings and not even the Chinese, who lined chartreuse robes with burning pink, ever dreamed such explosive colour combinations.

For your first Gaudy Asaphis Day choose some mangroves. Walk beside a long line of black, gray rocks near those mangroves. Look for broken bits of chipped, blackened, tarred shells along the rocks, or along the edge of muddy sand near the rocks. Revolting shells - that's what I look for first, probably hundreds of years old - mouldy and rotten. If you see some of these **STOP**. You have arrived. You need to consider something carefully.

You need to consider that Gaudy Asaphis are the cunningest camouflagers in the world of sea shells. Rock is black, right? Asaphis are dazzling orange or purple or yellow. So they should be easy to see, right? Wrong.

You can stare at a flamingo coloured shell lying on top of a black prickly rock for 15 minutes straight, and not see anything at all except black prickly rock. So don't look for this shell. Don't. Look for **THE COLOUR** of this shell - just a speck of colour hiding along an edge of rock. If you see a speck of colour bend down and look more closely. Sometimes you have to dig. Most of the time, you cannot move the rock. The rock is attached to half an island. Therefore, when you see your shell, very carefully whisk away the sand from underneath him. Once he is free you can ease him slowly from out of his hiding place.

If I want to have a Lucky Day, I walk along the entire territory of the Gaudy Asaphis in one direction. This territory is usually very small. I look carefully at all the **BLACK ROCK**. Then I retrace my steps in the other direction, and look carefully at **ALL THE SAND** in front of the black rock. If the shells which I have found are spectacularly beautiful, I make one more trip wading **THROUGH THE WATER** at a distance of about one foot from the black rock.

If you do all these things, you have got it made. On your first day, a gifted, much practiced adult sheller will probably find at least five very good shells. Your own three year old will probably find ten, and you - if you are an adult - will surely find one. If you do, and I am only talking about a perfect specimen, you will have begun a life long love affair with the Gaudy Asaphis, one you will remember with bliss every time you move him to a new location on your Perfect Tray.

## NUCLEUS SCALLOPS, ATLANTIC BITTERSWEETS, CARRIER SHELLS AND ORANGE TULIP MUSSELS

are often buried in that black nasty seaweed I described as lying one or two feet under water near a beach. Sometimes you can walk along three miles of beach covered with dried seaweed and never see a shell. Never. While only 50 feet further along, you will find another kind of underwater seaweed which day after day yields hundreds. The right seaweed, its cloudy bulk appearing like some black sea snake through 2 feet of water, is your tell-tale clue to all of the above shells.

## MUSSELS

Rocks do not usually gleam orange or purple. Dive, bend down, use a toe, or a Cockle Catcher for any orange or purple rock covered with algae in the shape of a Mussel. Mussels are almost always found in the same place, usually in clear sand, under three to four feet of water, sometimes gently rolling back and forth with the tide.

## HAWK-WING, MILK CONCH, AND ROOSTER-TAIL CONCHS

rarely reside on Outside Beaches. Inside sand flats are the places to search if these shells are your quest for the day. Hunting an area three miles by three miles is very tiring if one is only looking for lips and gleams, funny shaped rocks and poky up things. But if just one of them turns into a beautiful Rooster-tail Conch all that exercise will prove gratifying.

## MEASLED COWRIES

My best Measled Cowrie I found during a huge storm after one of my worst four mile walks along an Outside Beach. A piece the size of a dime winked in the sun. In a disgusted and exhausted frame of mind, I poked around with my big toe. A bottle I presumed. My toe hesitated after a second. Was it a bottle? On p.158 regard with awe what my wondering fingers finally dug up in frantic, unbelieving haste.

## SEA FANS

You might find a Sea Fan anywhere after a storm,. Once you know where the waves usually wash them, you can return year after year to those same places. High up rocks edging isolated prickly islands are favourite Sea Fan places.

## CRABBIES

I find these drying in the sun on the top of seaweed. I find them on the sand. Sometimes they are floating on the water. Crabbies live everywhere. If your Crabbie is already dry, it is better not to wet him. He usually disintegrates. If he is already wet, put him in his own little container for your returning voyage. Once home arrange him carefully into an attractive Crabbie position and let him dry in the sun. If you try to rearrange a dry Crabbie, he will probably break in half. If he is missing an eye or a leg, I would not add him to my collection. For me Crabbies must be perfect.

## BABY SHELLS

My best beach for finding babies is a 200 foot curve Inside a tiny, uninhabited island. Babies cover yards at a time on one of the beaches of this island. While attempting the perfect find, it is restful to lie down with a small child at your side helping you. If the shells are so small that your eyes are having a difficult time deciding which ones to choose, scoop up jarfulls and examine them the next day at your leisure. A magnifying glass helps. A small child helps most.

I can still remember the triumph of an excited child's voice "Mummy, Mummy - look - a Baby Turkey's Wing." That was the first Baby Turkey Wing we had ever seen. I noticed guests peering at a one eighth inch shell, held up in the proudest small palm, turning puzzled eyes to each other thinking, "Is this family mad?"

## FLAT CALM DAYS AND KING HELMETS

One of the world's most beautiful shell faces belongs to a King Conch. It is exquisitely brown or mirrored orange, (what shell books call a King Helmet or what scientists refer to as a Cassis tuberosa Linné). It is almost impossible to find. What is easier to look for is a dark six inch rock in the shape of a small triangular mountain. Most rocks are not shaped like mountainous triangles. Even if his salmon coloured flesh greets you with a terrified slurp, after you have picked him up, he is still worth a jump out of your boat and you will not feel sad. Surely one day you will find another one who has just recently suffered a major heart attack.

King Conchs live in two to four feet of water at Low Tide. We only find them on flat calm days. Usually the empty shell of a King Conch is so perfect you can't help wondering how he died. Did he get sick? Did the Hunter who ate him use a vacuum cleaner snout?

Sometimes, after raging storms, if you dig around small buried mountains at the base of rock conglomerations high upon a beach, you might be happily surprised. Usually, alas, beach specimens are exactly the way shell books describe them - sad spectres of might-have-been. However, a triangular rock under three feet of ocean is a different matter altogether.

## RAMS HORNS

Find an Outside Beach. Look for sand dunes, Casuarina trees, and stalks of grass which are long and brown and seem to be overladen wheat bending in the wind. Somewhere along that beach, about 100 feet inland, amidst orange vines that scratch your legs and invisible prickles that pierce your toes, a person can find hundreds of Rams Horns. Restless dead leaves under this bush or that hide Spirula spirula - perfect ones. Inside Beaches also have them, but not in such concentrated numbers as Outside Beaches. If you do not need hundreds of Spirula spirula for your treasure trays, try displaying them inside wine glasses.

If you remember the location, year after year, when you return you are likely to discover more. If, however, those carpets of brown leaves are disappointingly empty, and hiding places under bushes seem unaccountably blank, notice which way the wind is blowing. A strong wind blowing out to sea may have whipped away all your longed for Spirula spirula.

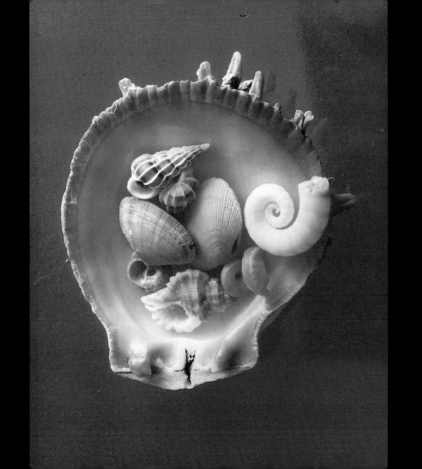

# CHAPTER IX

# BY THE LIGHT OF

# THE MOON

"And hand in hand, on the edge of the sand,

They danced by the light of the moon,

The moon,

The moon,

They danced by the light of the moon."

It seems to me that as a Caribbean Full Moon stirs nameless longings in all save the most insensitive heart, so it must also hold some strange fascination for shells.

I am not sure what happens during Full Moon nights. Do shells gather together in wild exultation? Do they feast in orgies of Bacchanalian celebration? In the froth of moon glittering waves, do they dance cotillions of love? Who can tell?

Suffice it to say that at Low Tide, on Full Moon days, when the ocean seems to have drawn impossible leagues from the shore, when the water bares secret places in the centre of vast, far away seas, shells appear which I never see at any other time of the month.

Once I found four Carrier Shells, cunningest babies, side by side with two sturdy granddaddies. Once I found a Hawk-wing Conch, Strombus raninus, (not the dwarf variety which is the common variety where I live, but full grown and as big as a Milk Conch, the only one I have ever seen). He was stranded with the most beautiful of Carrier Shells high up on the beach - or so I thought. Carefully I put the poor darlings back in the water.

For three days I returned to these unforgettable shells. My mouth watered. Temptation was almost irrepressible. They were such perfections - perfect Carrier, perfect raninus. I wanted them, I needed them - especially the raninus. When you have never seen a shell before, yearning is tripled, quadrupled into an almost over mastering passion.

Every day each shell had climbed perhaps 16 feet beyond the low water mark. Why? Poor angels, roasting alive in the sun. Carefully, I returned them to the coolness of their natural habitat.

Upon the fourth day, my beloved Hawk-wing Conch had disappeared entirely, and the Carrier Shell was stinking carrion. I thought I had coveted him, needed him. How contrary we humans. Now I felt sad. Perhaps my craving had killed him. I started to wash away the putrid mess, wrinkling my nose in disgust. Imagine my horror to notice huge bristle worms sludging along out of this shell - fat, bulgy, bristly, two or three inch long invaders. They were dead. Had there been a battle? Had they killed Mr. Carrier? Had Mr. Carrier climbed each day with pain and difficulty high upon the sand to lie in that merciless sun, knowing it was a question of who was going to die first? Was I unknowingly a Murderer - I whose altruistic image of myself had always been Angel of Mercy?

I will never know. What I do know is that, for me, Full Moon Days are the most exciting days of any month. I always see signs of strange shell happenings. Murder has occurred during the night, but what kind of murderer **ONLY** attacks extraordinarily coloured Cockles? I often notice brand new varieties of shell, and when I do, I wonder if they also have been unable to resist some siren call of Temptation,

"Leave your holes just tonight, only for one night.  Pray come.  To the dance mes chères."

I like to imagine that maybe Death, sad though it is, was perhaps one last ecstasy of Communion with the Moon, the gladness of welcoming her magnificence worth any risk of exposure.  So might we all wish to die, in love, exalting, passionate - the bodies we leave behind tantalizing, uncracked hymns to the passing of one perfect night.

# CHAPTER X

# DANGERS

## BARE FEET

It seems to me that many lives suffer from lack of Physical Danger. The older we grow, the more we tend to build safer, tidier, higher fences of protection around us. But Danger survived, Danger met and outwitted by our own individual skill, provides a thrill which adds dimension to all we do ever afterwards. Even in little things. Barefoot things.

Here is a chart to consider when you are deciding, "Yes you will wear shoes", or "No you will not wear shoes", as you start off each morning of your beginning-to-be-passionate Shell Game.

### CHART FOR CONSIDERATION
### OF
### BARE FEET VS. SHOES

| BARE FEET | SHOES, SNEAKERS OR BEST OF ALL BOOTIES |
|---|---|
| Nothing extra to carry | Something extra to carry |
| At night if you clean your feet first, before entering your little boat, your little boat stays clean. | Older people will not take off their shoes before stepping into your little boat. Since you often are younger than they are, you feel diffident about asking such a favour. If they do not remove their shoes, nothing you do will clean them. Each night the resulting chaos will cover your little boat with wretched tar, and fill your bed with bushels of sand. |
| Pleasure of Freedom. Feel the water. Feel the sand. | No pleasures. Stifling, suffocating, squelchy horrors. Sand scrapes and rubs against all your protesting skin. |
| At night - feet aching and lacerated with cuts a possibility. | At night - feet feeling lovely and refreshed. Secret gloating over perfect feet. |

People playing any kind of Shell Game in the South Pacific need shoes. First of all there isn't any sand except in the Maldives. Ground up rock is what there is, cut-your-feet-to-ribbons coarsely ground up pebbles. Not sand.

Second of all, things in the South Pacific kill you dead. Stone Fish kill you; Cone Shells kill you; and so do Blue Spotted Octopuses. In the Exumas there are things which will hurt you, sting you, slash you, cut you, pierce you, and bite you, but nothing is likely to kill you, if you take reasonable precautions in a spirit of resourceful adventurousness.

Within a few weeks of walking barefoot everywhere you go, you will develop hard and wonderful soles to your feet. If you do not have a few weeks, then particular care is necessary all the time.

### GRAY ROCKS FULL OF GHASTLY PRICKLES

This is the worst kind of rock. If you are barefoot do everything in slow motion. Put a foot down if it looks safe. Very slowly add pressure to see if you can stand the pain, and also to see if the rock is going to break . If you cannot stand the pain, or if the rock is going to break, choose another place. **BE CAREFUL.** Most people do not walk across this kind of rock. Pareos are marvelous inventions. If you have gone half way across your area of rock, and you wish that you had not, lay your pareo down in front of you. Walk across it. Pick it up. Do this again. Soon you will have reached the other side, and, returning, you could always swim home.

### LOW TIDE LONG STRETCHES OF BROWN WET SOFT ROCK

Nice, smooth, soft, weed-covered rock just emerging from the surf can change into sharp agonizing prickles with absolutely no difference in appearance to the untutored eye. Always be suspicious of this kind of rock. Never look up unless you are standing perfectly still. Not only can this kind of rock change into prickles, but far worse, instantaneously it can become slippery as ice. Whenever I see a Low Tide brown rock jutting out of the water, I try to avoid it. This is difficult because its coolness is so inviting to tired feet. If you can think about Ulysses bound to his mast, frantic to join those tempting sirens, it will be easier for you to find an alternative route.

### PEN SHELLS

The Amber Pen Shell (Pinna carnea), secretes a thread, or byssus, down to some firm anchorage from which it grows upwards. Its top is a quarter fan shape, often covered with weed, sometimes appearing above water at dead Low Tide. Its bottom is a point stuck sharply into greyish grass. It is pale orange. In ancient times, and even as late as 1914, people of the Mediterranean used to weave material as exquisite as the lightest silk called, "Cloth of Gold" from its byssus.

As a rule, Amber Pen Shells live in little areas of grass growing in sludgy sand. At low tide these areas often have a terrible odour. The grass is sometimes sparse and sometimes thick. Always look ahead when you are walking. It is not wise to put one foot into this murk until you have seen and studied many Amber Pen Shells.

one foot into this murk until you have seen and studied many Amber Pen Shells. Grass covered areas usually sprout hundreds of these enemies. A Pen Shell's greenish, darkish, blackish line is shaped like this:

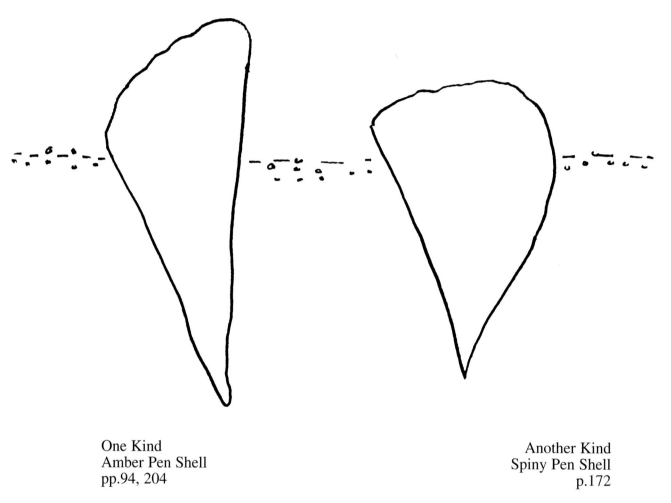

One Kind
Amber Pen Shell
pp.94, 204

Another Kind
Spiny Pen Shell
p.172

Once you know an Amber Pen Shell you will immediately recognize it on days when the water is clear. But even I, the world's most passionate advocate of bare feet, never step into a grassy area on stormy, gray-water days without exercising the most incredible caution.

Do not be afraid. Luckily such stormy days seldom last for long in the Exumas. And once you know what to look for, you will never forget. Recognizing an Amber Pen Shell is like riding a bicycle. Our family calls Pen Shells, "Razor Shells" because, although innocuous looking, their tops cut as surely as two inch wide razor blades. Always look carefully from your boat before you hop over the edge if you are hopping. Always imagine that if you step squarely onto a Pen Shell your bare foot will be cut right in half.

Children are much quicker than adults. Once they are taught what to look for, they seldom make mistakes. They have very bright eyes. I believe children should be allowed to do more, allowed to risk more, and be less protected. You just have to tell them calmly and clearly once. Then it becomes a game. They look after you as you walk to shore. Gleefully they point out horrid menaces along the way in case your old eyes don't see so well any more.

My old eyes of 28, (which is when I first came to the Bahamas with my babies), were not nearly as sharp as those of my three, four and five year olds, none of whom could swim, and all of whom used to yell out,

"Watch it Mummy, Razor Shell dead ahead."

## BARRACUDAS

My husband says that barracudas do not bite. I do not like them. They are usually long and gray in shape; they are not nice. My husband says they come in close to shore because they are curious. When their mouths go in and out as if they were panting, with those huge teeth just waiting to try out some succulent flesh, I don't care if they are curious or not. I back slowly from the beach, and talk to myself severely so I won't succumb to hysterics.

When I am swimming across a cut between sandbanks during a falling tide, I am not terribly nervous. But if the tide is rising, I am constantly searching for a long, gray, shadow nosing in for a bite. I hate him. He is almost always there in various lengths. If you feel as I do, take someone along for the swim  - the bigger, the stronger, the tougher the someone the better. The knowledge that Barracudas never attack humans is no comfort at all, if you have reached the middle of a cut and suddenly you are face to face with this devil. I would much rather meet a little shark than a big Barracuda. Most of all, I would much rather be able to touch bottom or be swimming on an Outside Beach if the tide is rising. **DURING RISING TIDES, FISH HUNT**. I don't mind them hunting, but I don't like them hunting me.

## STING RAYS

Sting Rays show up vividly in clear, shallow water. They resemble great black platters which stay very still, and seem as if they might be rocks. But why are these rocks so black, so evenly formed, and so flat? After you have asked yourself this question look for a long black stick attached to your rock. If you find the stick, it is a good bet that it is a tail, and that the rock is a Sting Ray. If the stick and rock move together you can be certain they are not a stick and a rock. Some Sting Rays are small and black; some Sting Rays are huge and black. Almost all Sting Rays avoid people. I like them. They remind me of beginnings. "In the Beginning God created the heaven and the earth . . ." I never look at one without thinking of Peter Mathiessen's *The Tree Where Man was Born*.

Another kind of Sting Ray lives in shallow, sun baked flats. Watch out. He is not another kind of Sting Ray; you just think he is. That's because he is not black. He

sticking out from the white flat rock all over again. Since you and the Sting Ray are both in about eight inches of water, and since this time you are miles from shore, and since, if you, like me, are barefoot, this is scary - quite scary in fact. The reason Mr. Sting Ray is white is because he is buried in sand. He isn't really buried, however. He has merely covered himself with just enough sand to receive a gentle suntan, but luckily without quite enough sand to entirely obliterate his general outline.

Sometime I cannot find his tail. But if I do not see a tail and am still a little suspicious about white, dusty, submerged platters, I look carefully around their edges to see if I can find two little humps laid close together. These two little humps will probably prove to be eyes looking unnervingly straight at you. These eyes are only hard to find if this is your first sun bathing sting ray.

Over a mile from shore, I never walk on sand flats covered with water against the sun. I want the sun at my back so that I can see any dangers along my route. Once I am sure of a Sting Ray I back off, and make a quiet little detour. He was there first. If, however, he is lying close to a perfect Gaudy Asaphis, I don't detour. Slowly I shuffle my feet, and hope he gets the message that I am momentarily in need of his territory.

## BLUE CRABS
are huge Prehistoric Monsters. Mangroves are where one sometimes finds Speckled Tellins and sometimes West Indian Chanks. Mangroves are full of the stickiest, most foul smelling mud. Easily you can sink into it above your knees. Unfortunately mangroves are also home to Blue Crab fiends, who, when they stick out all their legs, measure two feet across.

The second you see one zooming straight at you, you do not feel well if you are a lady. I don't know what men do, but I do know what I do. I scream. Loudly. I HATE Blue Crabs - especially when they chase you for afternoon tea.

## POISON BUSH
Poison Bush is nasty. It is a bush or a tree depending upon its age. It has dark green, menacing leaves, curly at the edges, which hang down in a drooping fashion. These are lined with bright yellow veins, and are sometimes astonishingly shiny. If you touch poison bush anywhere, or even one of its fresh leaves upon the ground, within one or two days you will wake up feeling logy. An area of skin not even as big as a 25¢ piece, and sometimes not much bigger than two or three pin heads stuck together, will swell. In the beginning it turns red. You will not believe that something so small can be driving you so wild. It itches. You feel sick. You itch all over, not just in the area of this one spot. Sometimes you itch under the arms and in the groin. If you grimly spray the spot four or five times a day with spray such as I mention on p.37, or else use the marvelous new gels also mentioned, AND DO NOT SCRATCH AT ALL, after three or four days the symptoms begin to disappear. An antihistamine at night is also helpful.

If you scratch your Poison Bush, dear sheller, yelling at me, "But the itch is insane", you will probably have to go to a hospital. Going to a hospital from a boat in the Exumas is complicated. Great water blisters can cover your stomach, your legs, and your arms. If they do you will carry their scars for the rest of your life. The easiest solution in the beginning is, "No Scratching".

Did I hear someone say, "But I'm Shelling. I'm not touching Poison Bush. I'm looking for **SHELLS**. Why do I want to go into the bush?"

Hmmmmmmmm . . . what occurs when you are on one beach murmuring to yourself, "See that beach over there, just around the corner, if I just climb these few rocks and travel around those isolated trees . . . "?

## REEFS

If I could dive, and if I wanted to inspect those perfect dead shells in the ooze which Mr. Humfrey, in his incredible *Sea Shells of the West Indies,* describes at the base of certain reefs, I would wear:

> cotton gloves
> a long sleeve shirt
> cotton trousers
> and rubber feet which we call "booties".

I would wear all of these in addition to my diving jacket. Coral cuts are the slowest healing, the most easily infected, and the most painful cuts around. Why risk one all for the trouble of finding a few clothes? The trouble of healing a few coral cuts will prove infinitely greater.

## PEOPLE

They seem a funny danger. Well, supposing the Shell Game captures your imagination. You are lukewarm in the beginning, but little by little you say to yourself, "Hmmm there's more to this than meets the eye."

You begin to love your times with the Ospreys, the silver fish leaping in the sun, the blue tailed frisky lizards coming to call. You begin to reverence life in a way you were not expecting. You decide fish have feelings. They should die **quickly**. They should **NOT** flap around inside empty garbage pails because a fisherman tells you, "Oh that's just reflexes". You know it's <u>not</u> reflexes, because when you cut the head off of your fish he never flaps again.

I once had a Scientist friend, a man of courtly old world charm peculiarly attentive to the confidings of children and other important people. I never knew that when scientists collect in wild, inaccessible parts of the world, they collect thousands and thousands of living shells, putting them into drum after drum of something which smells like formaldehyde.

At the end of each day, I had to hand over my beauties instead of hiding the creatures away so that nobody could ever find them again. This was a new game for me.

"We are his helpers."

"It's for science. Science needs you to help him. He's old."

"Why don't you grow up?"

It didn't matter what I said to myself, slowly, as day followed day, even if I was aiding and abetting the important work of Science, I began to feel physically ill. The quality of South Pacific Light no longer held the same allure. Who cared about the song of some strange bird? My footsteps lagged upon beaches totally alien to the Exumas. Banging the heads of inquisitive sharks with a bamboo pole as they darted in, curious to inspect my ankles or knees, was no longer a heroic, "I'm a heroine, watch me, watch me - eh Les Requins", shouting, hilarious game. As for shells, I became sick at the thought of them. They nauseated me. For three whole months of a continuing voyage in a sailboat, I completely avoided them, and as for my lovely-going-to-sleep-reading shell books, searching new facts, relishing new names like Hippopus hippopus or Harpa harpa - out the nearest porthole with all that junk. Those three months were bad months.

Again in the Exumas once upon a time, I had another sort of friend. A very intellectual solver of very important, crucial world problems. I don't mean he wanted to solve them, the way I do with a sort of hopeless feeling of despair, he did solve them. He was equipped with the mind and the training to succeed.

He did not pooh pooh aqua turning to green, frothing white baby waves skedaddling to shore in laughable imitation of their granddaddies; he did not ridicule baby Ospreys trying and hopelessly trying again to utter those clear haunting notes of Mummy and Daddy, he just did not notice; he didn't revel; he wasn't quiet as if he were in a church.

All the important things which were happening to his world: over-population, famine, starvation, diminishing oil supplies, pollution, sent out such vivid flashing sparks that of course these lesser Exuma teeny voices were electrocuted in the process.

"Shells - you're not serious - Shells??? Are **SHELLS** important?"

He didn't condemn. He would never dream of condemning someone's else's private little hobby. He was much too warm and too polite for that kind of cruel murder. He was amazed - that's all. So amazed, so genuinely startled, he couldn't help showing it.

This type of person should be savoured to the full in other surroundings. This type of person is very, very dangerous to players of the Shell Game. What he unconsciously thinks becomes an insidious time bomb ticking away, erupting suddenly, or killing slowly by radiation. How or where doesn't matter. It's the "when" which is excruciating. For me this time around was the worst. I avoided shells for two whole years after my friend's visit. Now I am wiser. Experience has taught me. I hesitate before sharing my fascination. Instead, with each new batch of guests, I wait around and see. I am looking for a kindred spirit, a rejoicer in the wilderness. I organize the sailors, the windsurfers, the water-skiers, the frisbee players, the talkers, and maybe even join in. All these things have great charm, but during my organizing or joining, I am always watching. I am looking carefully at each eager three year old, every contemplative eighty year old. Intently my eyes are asking, "Excuse me, but are you a Kindred Spirit?"

At just the right second, hardly mentioning the incredible excitement of our forthcoming adventure except in a low key, "I've learned my lesson" way, myself and my choice of heart zoom off together to rejoice and sing out, "Oh look", and muse aloud, and explore and . . .

"Oh Cécile isn't this <u>exactly</u> like a Treasure Hunt?"

Ha! Then I can smile secretly, and know that I have really found a Kindred Spirit.

Solomon exhorted us to consider a lily and how it grows. Someone Else said,

"To everything there is a Season and to everything a Time and Place."

A lily in a field in front of the Allied Armies marching into Germany at the end of World War II caused no one's detour. And yet, consideration of a lily in some quiet, reflective moment contributed to King Solomon's legendary wisdom, and could contribute to ours, if we would listen, if we knew enough to pick up a live shell with reverence, summoning the courage to balance our covetous lust with these questions:

"Do I need this for science?"

"Am I a serious, serious collector?"

# CHAPTER XI

# IDENTIFICATION

Take a shell book - any shell book.  Open it to any page and read things like:

> "Moderately thin periostracum."
> "Pustulated Parietal shield."
> "Sculpture of Axial growth lines."
> "Numerous rounded costae."
> "Extensive brown maculations."
> "The whorls are shouldered . . ."

The words pound in your mind.  Are you dumb or something?  What's a costae?  What's a periostracum?  Pustulated - does that mean oozing like a sore?  Of course not - these are shells.  Is the shield Outside or Inside?  Axial.  Let's see - the world has an axis.  Does axial mean straight up and down?  Straight up and down what?

How big is the dictionary?  How heavy is the dictionary?  How far away is the dictionary?  How much do you need to know the name of your shell?

There are a lot of questions you have to ask yourself when you find a shell whose name does not immediately spring to mind.  For weeks you settle for Helmet.  It is either a King Helmet or a Princess Helmet.  It might even be a Queen Helmet but, until recently, where I live no one has ever found one so I tend to concentrate on Kings and Princesses.

At least the English name seems to be Princess, but the Latin is Cassis flammea.  Maybe we should forget Princesses and talk about Flames.  Except that in the Bahamas the fishermen call this shell Princess.

> "See dis here Princess conch?  Ma'm you trades us some grits for
> dis here Princess?"

How about babies on beaches?  If you have a baby Cassis flammea which, at about one inch in length, is one of the world's most adorable shells, and a baby King Helmet or Cassis tuberosa, and you found both of them on the same beach on the same day how do you tell the difference?  Baby Shells are tough to identify.

For three nights this author fell asleep in frustrated desperation after juggling weighty volumes around her bed until finally she dumped the whole cascade of books all over her recumbent and protesting husband.

> "You find this dumb shell's name.  I'm sick of it.  You went to
> Harvard.  I didn't.  Harvard should teach shells.  Shells are
> important.  **NOW WORK!**"

Very patient with his volatile wife, her husband looked surprised for a moment and then read quietly.  After fifteen minutes of pondering he asked mildly,

> "Cécile, what does reticulated mean?"

"Who cares? Who cares what dumb reticulated means? Who wants to care? It's stupid, stupid, stupid. Just tell me the difference. I just want to know the different names for the two different shells, and I do <u>not</u> want to know what Reticulated means."

"Cécile, get the dictionary. Look up the word reticulated, and maybe I'll tell you which is a baby King Helmet and which is a baby Princess Helmet. Maybe I will, and maybe I won't. Now move."

"Reticulated - 'a fine network of lines'."

Ah ha! So if the baby has fine crisscrossing lines all over it, it is a Cassis tuberosa or King Helmet, and if it is shiny and smooth and just has thicker lines curving in one direction, or no lines, and certainly not a <u>network</u> of lines, it is a Cassis flammea or Princess Helmet.

Of course, if it is a fully grown shell, it is easy to tell because a King Helmet is big, and a Princess Helmet is little. An adult King Helmet has a triangular face, and an adult Princess Helmet's face has one of its triangular edges rounded instead of pointed. A mature King Helmet's crisscross of lines has changed into hundreds curving in one direction, all close together. A mature Flame Helmet has hardly any lines. So big shells are easy. But I love baby shells, and nobody ever explains them to me.

They do too Cécile. You just don't want to master the terms Science has invented for the study of shells.

No. I want English.

It is English. It is just English above your head.

Could we get to The Emperor?

## LIMPETS

Oh Limpets of the seas. Limpets clinging to rocks, but never in my sight. Limpets just after storms. Wonderfully fascinating Limpets. It has taken me three years of Christmas Vacation research to sort out Limpets. Truly, I am proud to announce that I can tell you a few interesting things about Limpets not explained in simple English in most shell books.

Limpets have undeniable charm. Keyhole Limpets have holes. In Latin they are called Fissurellidae. True Limpets have no holes. Their Latin name is Acmaeidae.

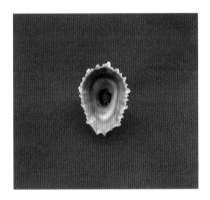

All around the **INSIDE** of this Barbados Keyhole Limpet curve horizontal concentric lines of various shades of green. The strength of the green depends upon the newness of the shell. If you look at the **OUTSIDE** of a Barbados Keyhole Limpet, you will notice that there are **ELEVEN** large, distinctive lines starting at the hole of the shell and traveling in a vertical fashion towards the bottom of the shell. Two of the lines, at one end of the shell, are much, much closer together than the even spacing of all the other lines.

Barbados Keyhole Limpet
Fissurella barbadensis
Gmelin, 1791

On the outside of the Wobbly Keyhole Limpet, there are many fine red lines radiating in a vertical fashion from the hole to the base of the shell. If you put this Limpet on a flat surface, you can rock him forward and backward, forward and backward, like a rocking chair. If he doesn't rock he isn't a Wobbly Keyhole Limpet.

Wobbly Keyhole Limpet
Fissurella fascicularis
Lamarck, 1822

The outer white lines of the Knobby Keyhole Limpet have much deeper valleys between them than the Barbados Keyhole Limpet. If the Limpet is not too worn, he has spectacular little knobs adorning these lines. It is hard to find a perfect, unchipped Knobby Keyhole Limpet. Mine are white.

Knobby Keyhole Limpet
Fissurella nodosa
Born, 1778

Do you think this Lister was a relation of the English Dr. Lister who invented the world's first antiseptic? I call this Limpet my dancing lady's dress Limpet. The "strong concentric threads" on the outside of this shell form such exquisitely fine little squares that an admirer can't help imagining some Southern Belle whirling towards Queen of the Evening in her latest Diodora listeri.

Lister's Keyhole Limpet
Diodora listeri Orbigny, 1853

Now you know that a Diodora listeri is not a Barbados Keyhole Limpet because Barbados Keyhole Limpets are horizontally green inside. Remember? A Diodora listeri is white, cream, or gray inside. Also the Diodora listeri has many more lines, or radial ribs, on its outside than eleven, some of them thick and heavy. Also, although beach specimens are bleached pure white, newer Diodora listeri have seven or eight blotches of green at the edges of their skirts. Their outside color is not diffused all over, like the brown speckles of barbadensis. It seems to come in clumps.

Cancellate Fleshy Limpet
Lucapina suffusa
Cancellate
Reeve, 1850
Freshly dead pale pink,
or, on your left, bleached
white by the sun.

Before he is faded by the sun into pure white, a pale pink of early morning sky suffuses the body of Lucapina suffusa Reeve. The hole at the top of this shell is often a circle of smashing dark gray hue. It is impossible to confuse Lucapina suffusa Reeve with any of these other Limpets because he is so much more fragile and delicate. The other shells in this discussion have heavier more forceful lines. Lucapinas are rare and finely etched as if Dürer's pen had lightly drawn their markings. Anybody who loves Limpets will become very attached to Lucapina suffusa Reeve otherwise known as a

Fleshy Limpet.

On the next rainy day - luckily Bahamian Rain doesn't last very long - harassed parents could easily pass out pretty coloured paper napkins, shirt cardboard, and glue to all of their children. The children could then make their own shell boards to adorn their bedroom walls. Gluing the paper napkin to cardboard - if the napkin is the heavy kind - creates a lovely background which handles ink and glue beautifully. Limpets are just the right weight for gluing. Elmer's wash-off glue harms nobody. The children can practice their best handwriting labeling each Limpet. This part of the Shell Game is very addictive to very young children just learning to write. They are so pleased with their final effects, wanting to look at them again and again.

# BITTERSWEETS

The beaks of these shells, (the pointing parts), are centrally located and point towards each other. The Atlantic Ocean is in the centre of two land masses. That is how you can remember that the beaks of the Atlantic Bittersweet are **CENTRED**.

Atlantic Bittersweet
Glycymeris undata
Linné, 1758
Straight beaks

The beaks of these shells are **OFF CENTRE**, and curve to the left. P.196 of one of my favourite paperbacks, *Seashells of North America*, by R. Tucker Abbott, says that they "point posteriorly".

Decussate Bittersweet
Glycymeris decussata
Linné, 1758
Crooked beaks

## BABIES AND JUVENILES

In so many cases babies and juveniles are so absurdly unlike adults that never ever would a Beginning Sheller put the two together. A baby Measled Cowrie is paper thin, long and narrow, made of a see-through, palest beige. When he is a teenager, he has dark lines on him. Only when he finally grows up does his aperture curve inwards and his teeth come out all in a neat row. Only an adult sprouts spots of startling beauty (p.158).

**QUEEN CONCHS**
Strombus gigas Linné, 1758

Baby Conchs, often called "rollers" in the Bahamas, are such small babies nobody would dream they could ever grow up.

Teenager conchs are an acceptable size but of only mild beauty with no flaring lip.

The lips of young adult conchs flare in fluted surfaces of rarest porcelain. Their colours of sunset pink and orange are so extraordinary that you might have to check out your first find several times a day.

The Queen. Truly the Queen in all her maturity has no rival. Her lip is thicker now - rich and mature. Curtsy lesser shells. Your Queen has arrived.

Grandma & Grandpa. Ah age. To each of us it comes. Our boat doesn't eat old conch. We use it for catching fish. Fish don't like it much either. The lips of old conch become heavy, worn away, old, and filled with worm holes. Feeling discouraged? Regard this unique hero.

With many shells, there is no easy way to mark the beginning, the middle, and the ending of their lives.  It is a subject bearing such complexity that one's mind is in a continual wrangle of, "It must be", "Well could it be?", "I know what it is."  At least these arguments provide diversions from one's feet which can't help protesting the trillion miles of trudging towards "just one more bend Mummy."

# CHAPTER XII

# SIDE EFFECTS

## NOT A MURDERER

It's fun. It's not fun murdering, not if you know how darling the little creature with his head poking out, nor how fair his flaring mantle.

Even the shiniest, most perfect, most incredible shell in the world - even the firm argument, "I'm only going to take one" of each species - even the fact that you're collecting for science and museums, cannot entirely erase that small pang of anguish which clutches your heart each time you and your murdered one are together.

> "He's dead because of me. He's soft. He's squishy. He's just a little animal, and he can make porcelain as exquisitely delicate as any Chinese two legged rival. Man still finds shells made before Man was born. I killed him. I killed him."

Sheller, to whatever degree you have ever felt any of these feelings, try playing this game, and wonder how quickly that hurtful nagging turns into satisfaction and triumph.

Most scientists state that Excellent Shell Collections require Death. Instead of Death your collection could speak of Perseverance and Cunning.

You, the hunter, followed clues which led you to the right place and the right time. Maybe you were just lucky. Perhaps you braved the wilds of a storm. However you won your prize, your journey was uncomplicated by murder.

## EXPANDING VOCABULARIES

People who have small vocabularies, if they are curious, cannot play this Shell Game without expanding their Word Horizons. In order to name some of their rarer finds, they will need a dictionary. Without knowing the meaning of "reticulated", it is difficult to guess with certainty a Baby Flame Helmet.

## INSOMNIACS

This Shell Game could be a soothing soporific for insomniacs. At night they would not have to be afraid of reading something that will wake them up even more. Identifying just one shell - using perhaps twenty minutes - could lull them into the deepest slumber.

## NO TELEPHONES - SUPPOSE YOU DECIDE TO PLAY THIS SHELL GAME FROM A BOAT - ALONE FOR A WEEK

When you make your first conscious decision to abandon telephones and people, it is difficult in the beginning. It's almost as if you can't. Not alone. Supposing you don't like yourself? But in the end, the Infinite beckons as willful and demanding as Man's strongest narcotic. When you and the Shell Game start up again each year, suddenly one day that "peace which passeth understanding" is yours. You have arrived, once more, at last.

## ARTIST

Each of us is creative. Most of us just don't have the time or the self confidence to begin. Beginnings so often resemble the pitiful scratchings of back yard hens that it is easy to give up in wry discouragement.

Absolutely nothing is discouraging, however, about one's first Sea Art arrangement. On the contrary it is thrilling. One Sea Fan masterfully hammered to your wall, one Conch in the middle of a table, one ancient and silvered Beach Bottle toted home by one little boy just beginning to think that maybe this game isn't for sissies after all, and the foundations of Impermanent Art have been laid. By filling his bottle with sand into which you stick Wild Beach Grasses, you have begun to unleash the Artist latent in your nature. As for the little boy, who can't tear his eyes away from <u>his</u> bottle in <u>your</u> collection, there is nothing "hen-scratchy" about his sudden importance.

A stationary table top is a fine Art Palette. A sea-going table top, or window sill or bookcase shelf, needing only a small ledge around it, is easily improvised with silver tape for a ledge, and your favourite plain towel for colour and stability. No matter how rough the day's sail, nor how many squalls deluge your motorboat, small shells stay put, and big ones can be moved back and forth at the beginning and the end of each day's traveling. I always found that the trouble, even when it lasted for two years, was well worth the strangely beguiling charm of even one of those seascapes.

Once you start, you never want to stop. Remembering even one of these creations soothes your mind with pleasure. Big Crabbies lecturing to audiences of Moon Snails - little Crabbies gathering within their Sea Fan school rooms - worm Shells, coiled in fantastic shapes, chatting politely with half open 'Coon Oysters clinging to sticks worn smooth by the ocean - the Queen of the Sea, Strombus gigas Linné 1758, watching over her realm with patient indulgence - babies nestled snugly into an Orange Spondylus cradle balancing upon all its points - Tulips inveigling fossilized Angular Tritons to join an afternoon tea party for juvenile Measled Cowries - the festivities becoming too hot, branches of delicate white coral wafting cool breezes. All of these images bring back rejuvinating moments - instant escape from Civilization's Confusion.

## IMPERMANENT ART

I once read about a young artist, Christo, who trailed miles of white nylon across the mountains of California, and then, standing back, vastly pleased with his creation, *The Running Fence*, promptly labeled it Impermanent Art.

Sometimes, however, you can't help becoming over involved. You never meant to spend so much time creating. But you see this shell needs a little more toothbrushing. What if you gave that shell just a lick of mineral oil? What do you think - does this Orange Spondylus holding babies look best, or how about a Magnum Cockle with all those pointed little edges for effect? Daily your interest grows. You can't help it. You are becoming hooked by this stupid Impermanent Art. (pp.134, 139)

You never knew it could be so interesting. Something else is growing though. Unease. Must the trip end? What about your Impermanent Art?


## PHOTOGRAPHY

is the answer. The experienced practitioner will be happy. He will be combining two fondnesses into one.

The Beginner, however, may be in for a paralysing shock. A lady I once knew was convinced that her camera could become a handsome, well set up little box easily able to shoot and record the colour of the light, the translucency of the shell exactly as it appeared to her musing eye in any given second of any day. Only after a desperate six months of unnerving failure did the words of her thirteen year old daughter, "Mummy, it's not so easy you know", begin to sink in.

Never mind. My husband's grandfather left all his descendants with this kernel of philosophy,

<blockquote>"Make stepping stones of your troubles."</blockquote>

A sensible boat has room for Time. Time in this instance means Shell Books and Photography Manuals.

With fast indoor film and practice, with a Macro Lens and maybe a collapsible tripod, one of your 100 pictures of Impermanent Art may be as great or greater than the original.

With outdoor film, you can take your camera to the beach. If nothing exciting occurs or if you are bored with your camera, you can leave it in its plastic bucket wrapped up a beach towel under some shady tree. Day after day you can do that. But - if today is your day for finding a perfect Rooster-tail Conch **ALIVE** - don't cry. Run back and fetch your camera. Take twenty pictures of the Find of the Day, if not the Find of the Year, and one picture is bound to remind you of Perfect Beauty on a Perfect Day found by a Perfect Good Samaritan.

## REJUVENATION

The Shell Game affords mighty release from too much too close - too many humans all crowded together in a boat which too often becomes a cockle shell of sandpapery walls. Off by yourself, searching away, there is time for recovery and little chats with God concerning the wonder of His Arrangements.

## THINNER

If you belong to that sad percentage of the world whose instincts to eat one more delicious morsel vie with a yearning to be thin, this Shell Game is a perfect game.

"And miles to go before I sleep,
And miles to go before I sleep."

Although Robert Frost was thinking of snow covered miles, the words are peculiarly suited to marching upon beaches, sinking into soft sandbanks, slogging through mangrove swamps. This exercise pays dividends. It yields up Treasures at the same time as legs become handsomer, tummies become flatter, and irretrievably lost face bones miraculously reappear.

## WIND CHIMES

My daughter is an artist. "But Mummy, Imperfection is also beautiful." She takes cracked shells, pretty coloured shells with holes in them, interesting shaped shells, and she strings them upon nylon fishing line attached to small pieces of exotic driftwoods. The wind, blowing through these creations, makes you never want to go home.

## GOOD SAMARITAN

A Good Samaritan . . . Does the Bible mention how nice his good deed made him feel? Being a Good Samaritan on the beach makes you sing songs you had forgotten. As you plunge each roasting, suffocating animal back into his ocean home is it only your imagination which listens to squelches of gurgling joy?

As for outthinking Murderers . . . A big shell is resting upon some clear white sand, in plain view of Mr. Live Sheller hurrying from around the nearest corner. Quick, hide him in some mushy seaweed; camouflage him near a shadowy mossy rock. At last Mr. Live Sheller passes by, and your living, perfect, unchipped, shiny, orange-lipped, enormous True Tulip is safe.

How gold then the sun, how beamingly he applauds your clever, life-giving action, how warm his words of praise as he seems to follow your retreating form with:
    "Bravo to stealth and quickness of mind oh Scarlet Pimpernal of the Day."

## NOT EVERYTHING THAT YOU COLLECT IS A SHELL

Sometimes I cross over to an Outside Beach to see what I can see. Sometimes I see the gorgeously unexpected, and sometimes what I see I can't take home. A shark all ominous, his fin sinuously cutting the mirror of some inland waterway, a barracuda torpedoing along, an eagle ray leaping, an Osprey, fish in talons for its young, swooping so low his breast feathers turn turquoise from the sea - these are some of the marvels which meet a questing eye.

Sometimes I eat a sardine, and if I am very still guests will come. Lizards with blue-green tails. Lizards are not very fond of sardines or carrots or cucumbers or peanut butter. I think they come to be polite. If I sit very still a lizard with his curled up tail will daintily try some sardine while perched upon my foot.

Sometimes I sleep awhile waiting for the tide. Banana birds seek out my pareo. Perhaps they think a flower fell upon their beach, but what is this arm, this leg? Their tiny claws inspecting my form provide me with one of those Passports into Paradise that so often and so unaccountably occur on most Shell Game days.

# CHAPTER XIII

# CLEANING

# THE PERIOSTRACUM
described by
William K. Emerson
as a "thin outer organic layer of skin"

**BITTERSWEETS** are covered with a charming, dark, furry covering - a kind of brown velvet softness.  The outsides of **ARKS** and particularly **MOSSY ARKS** are hidden by a hairy almost shaggy material.  Most **MUSSELS** have strands so roughly spaced their second skin seems, at times, to be entirely composed of large sand granules all stuck together in nasty clumps.

Amid the spines of **SPONDYLUS** wander white tubes of shell worms, or teeny sponges. Together with other types of deposits these create strange patterns.  After it has dried, the **SPINY COCKLE** is banded with ridges of what seems to be thin brown paper.

**GOLDEN COCKLES** are sometimes covered with a gray cloud or film - as if some master colourist had lightly painted over the brilliant oranges or yellows, the purples or browns.

The covering of **TUN SHELLS** is wetter and stickier, almost like a soft, dried mucus.

I don't know, I cannot tell - I am still not sure whether I like some shells better without their periostracum, (as this outer skin is called), or with it.  Some shells definitely improve; some shells seem more forlorn, as if they were missing something natural and proper.

You can patiently clean a cockle with your fingernail, or impatiently use a teflon cleaning pad.  The pad seems to work better with a minimum of water.  However, with the exception of the white cockle, at the end of all this labour, invariably I ask myself whether my shell is now more pleasing or not.

Cockles are for me a constant dilemma.  Perhaps it is an illusion, but even with the fingernail process, which is soft and natural, an orange cockle, without his gray painted-on-skin seems to fade much faster than when he remains in his original form.
In my opinion **TUN SHELLS** look better without their mucous outsides.

## CLEANING TOOLS
Some very successful cleaning tools for a boat are a thin wire brush about 1/4 inch in diameter, a stiff toothbrush, and a metal dental pick.  On a beach if you have come unprepared, and you can't wait another second, a soft stick or a fingernail works wonders.

I like the shapes which occur on the outsides of some shells - Arcs, Mussels and Bittersweets - so these I often leave in their natural state.  Other shells, such as Conchs or Tulips, I attack ruthlessly being very, very careful not to damage their lips.  Chipped lips are not allowed in my collection.

Cleaning a Conch aboard a boat is an invitation to disaster - boat and collector becoming deluged with masses of green algae.  Cleaning a Conch while standing in three feet of ocean, using a small stiff brush, is infinitely preferable.

## BOILING
You don't need to know about Boiling to play this kind of Shell Game.  Luckily.

## MURIATIC ACID AND FORMALDEHYDE
Sorry.  These two deadlies are out of my ken, and I wouldn't put any of my finds anywhere near either of them.

## BURY
If some of your just dead shells smell too foul for words, find some soft DRY sand 2' to 3' above the High Tide line.  Bury your Heart's Joy face, (or aperture) down.  Mark the spot with a stick or a rock.  Come back in a few days.  Ants and other scavengers will have performed their ancient task.  If you are so excited you forgot to bury your shell face down, the rotting liquid of the animal may run all over the shine of its front leaving horrid trails of burns or discolouration marks .  Unless you admire these acid tracks all you can do is throw away your shell.  Nothing will bring him back to his original condition.

## SUN
If you leave your brightly coloured, smelly shells in the hot sun hoping that the smell will go away, you will find, to your dismay, that the colour will diminish at about the same pace as the smell.

If, however, your white Coral, your white Sea Biscuits, your white Crabbies or white Starfish are not quite white enough, a few days of sun will prove a helpful tonic.

## SMELL
Pouring a few drops of alcohol or hydrogen peroxide into a badly smelling shell, and leaving it on a shelf for a few days is a technique which has been suggested to this author.  The trouble with doing this aboard a boat is that a boat is tippy.

## BLEACH
Bleach is a substance for which I have a profound respect.  I suggest you try it on one of your least important pieces.  I often fill my plastic bucket half full of sea water.  Sparingly I add a little bleach.  This solution is the Fountain of Youth for some of my more grey and dirty looking objects.

Twice a day I anxiously check whatever I am bleaching.  Sometimes I have to wait three impatient days and even add a tiny bit more bleach on the third day.

For Sand Dollars, Sea Eggs of all kinds and Sea Biscuits, bleach brings a new life - a rebirth.  For certain striped Sea Eggs which are an unappetizing greyish colour, the transformation from mundane to ethereal is astonishing.  What you thought were unappealing black ridges turn into rainbow lines of shadowy green and deep purple.

Sometimes you dig up pieces of **CORAL**.  The branches are a graceful shape.  The top is brilliant white.  But the bottom, where it has been buried in sand or seaweed, is a discordant brown.  This unhappy colour combination will cause pain to any avid collector, and is easily remedied by bleach.  But bleach how strong and for how long is The Question.  One hour, two hours, a day, two days?  Thinking about your specimen inside of your bleach bucket will quickly divert your mind from Trivia which used to seem Important.  Too strong bleach for too long will ruin your Coral.  Maybe bleach until you are nervous, and sun for several days afterwards will prove a valuable experiment.  I always use Sea Water along with my bleach because sea water is so plentiful aboard boats.

## BLEACH AND GOOD SHELLS

I don't like bleach for good shells. Every time I have looked at Coral incrustations whose shape I abhor, every time I have decided <u>not</u> to spend laborious hours with dental pick or stick removing growths or algae or hard deposits, and have gingerly plunged my latest ocean masterpiece into a bucket of bleach, even a weak solution of bleach, even for half an hour, the results have been catastrophic.

Books recommending bleach and muriatic acid for everything are written by practitioners more skilled than I am. My Best Shells, with the exception of what should be naturally white, stay out of bleach.

## HERMIT CRABS INSIDE YOUR SHELLS

Hermit Crabs do not look like shell animals. They have many scrabbling, wiggling legs. They are very active, and they crawl around, often wearing your best find of the day. When you peer inside their shell, seeing something hard, purple, and lifeless, beware of murmuring, "This shell is dead". You might be wrong. That hard purple colour might belong to a certain type of Hermit Crab Claw. Put your shell somewhere safe. Perhaps, in a little while, it will get up and walk away. It wasn't dead after all. Now begins your next problem.

You might say a Hermit Crab only borrowed his Sunflower Dress. It was created by somebody else. In a more ruthless mood, you could even say that he stole it. Therefore why not kill him? Although I am the best rationalizer around when it comes to excuses for doing what I don't wish to do, I find it hard work killing Hermit Crabs. I feel sorry for them.

In the South Pacific Tokelau Islanders showed us their solution. If they were right handed, they held their Hermit Crab shell in their left hand. Then they whistled, softly blowing onto the crab. Eventually, curious, the Hermit Crab would poke out his head. Quickly their right hand would grab his pincers, his feet, and as much of his head as they could manage. The ensuing tug of war had to be very gentle. It demanded steady nerves. When we first tried it, we broke Hermie in half, and it wasn't the rocking boat which made us all feel sick. Eventually, after you learn the trick, Hermie comes out whole, but it is a ticklish trick and not for queasy natures.

Another idea is to leave Hermie in a container with a new shell similar to the one you wish he would vacate. Sometimes he decides he likes that new home better than the one he is in, and off he goes on his Inspection Trip. Inspection means trying on. Once he has changed residence, I feel satisfied turning him loose upon the beach. But if Hermie is naked, I do not think it is fair to just abandon him without first making sure he has several suitable choices nearby. When Hermie is fresh and eager he is too clever to leave his shell. However, after he has been a prisoner for some hours, his cleverness turns into frustrated impotence, and he is willing to take chances he would never have dreamed of in the beginning.

The whole subject of Hermit Crabs bothers me a lot. It is nerve wracking to make a mistake and kill Hermie. In recent years, I do what I often do with insoluble problems. I avoid them. Let him keep his stolen shell. His shell is not worth my pain of waking up in the middle of the night, and seeing him all shriveled up and suffocated, or of remembering what a one half live Hermie looks like. He looks horrid, and he ruins my peacefulness.

Once, retiring from the scorching heat of the day into the cool of a wooded interior upon some far away and tiny islet, I could hardly believe my eyes.

## A HERMIT CRAB CONVENTION

Was that what I was seeing? Or maybe Orgies of Giant Copulation? Or perhaps I was witnessing an International Trade Fair for the Barter or the Comparison of Shells? In great rays from the center – sun extended outwards – thousands of gradated shells were rustling about. At their heart twitched a primordial creature – malevolent, huge and unseemly, with naked claws and body all hairy in dangerous shades of purple and red. They were worshipping so monstrous a ruler? These borrowed True Tulips, Apple Murexes, Milk Conchs, small Queen Conchs, Scotch Bonnets, and at their very periphery the tiniest of land snail shells?

If so, was I, by my physical presence, polluting the rhythms of Ancient Ceremony? No matter that I stopped instantly – willing my limbs into some new kind of contorted tree. No matter. They hated my astounded eyes. They felt my rigid silence. Scuttle, scuttle, scuttle – at first slowly, and then more and more rapidly, they rustled away to some hidden underbrush full of protective brown leaves for hiding places. As I stared at ground suddenly bereft of life, I found myself wondering all the more about hermit crabs, and all the more reluctant to become their murderer.

## COCKLES

When bivalves are wet and first fished from the Ocean Floor, sometimes they have a dead animal inside. This animal is droopy and floppy. If you are careful not to touch the hinge or ligament on the outside of the two shells, a dental pick is a perfect tool with which to gently remove the creature.

Now you have a decision to make. Is your Cockle more attractive closed into a ball, or do you prefer him half open? Maybe wide open is his prettiest position. "Which" is the decision you have to make while he is still wet. Because, 24 hours later, you cannot suddenly change your mind and say, "Hey - wait a minute - I made a mistake."

## CRABBIES

It is disastrous to try to clean a dry one by putting him back into the water. Don't. Use a dental pick instead to remove the sand, but do not wash him or he will disintegrate.

If you find a floating Crabbie or a Crabbie at the edge of the water line, in other words **A WET CRABBIE**, as soon as you arrive home, carefully arrange him in his most lifelike position.

Leave him to dry out and harden, and there he is - for years to come - a perfect Crabbie. He will smell in proportion to his size, but never for longer than a week. The trouble with putting him outdoors in the sun is that you forget him; the wind shifts, and you have lost your prize. For some a perfect Crabbie is a rare and sought after item.

## MINERAL OIL

Your shell came from the sea.  He was wet the day you found him.  The shine of rare jewels glowed from his surface.  The next morning you are no longer face to face with illusion.  The next morning he is dry, and
"naught but grief and pain for promised joy"

becomes your lot.

What to do?  You can use vaseline, baby oil, mineral oil.  They are especially helpful on the insides of Gaudy Asaphis.  However, by comparison to the REAL THING, these serve as camouflagers of mediocrity at best, and at worst they become horrid collectors of dust.

## FADING

Certain shells - for instance Cowries or Marginellas or Wide Mouth Purpuras seem to take years to lose their lustre, but, unfortunately, lose a lot they eventually do.  At least the process is a slow one.

As for Sunshells, Conchs, Cockles, Gaudy Asaphis - alas.  Brilliant oranges, amethyst purples, rays of the setting sun - colours to leap the heart with joy - nothing seems to maintain their brightness.  Inevitably when I return at Christmas a year later, rushing to greet my gems - oh sadness, oh dull Death dully saying, "Hello".  In place of heavenly brilliance, only the pale mockery of colour that was greets my eye.  All the above remedies applied in frantic, sorrowing haste, perhaps work for other collectors a year later, but for me they only intensify my impression of faded grandeur.

All I can do is feast my eyes every few seconds upon my most charming finds of the day consoling myself with Macbeth's bitter recognition that nothing lasts.
" Out, out, brief candle!

> Life's but a walking shadow, a poor player,
> That struts and frets his hour upon the stage,
> And then is heard no more; it is a tale
> Told by an idiot, full of sound and fury,
> Signifying nothing."

So we all feel on certain dreadful days when we rail against unmerciful fate.  Things end.  Roses die.  Wrinkles come.  So?  When the beauty of a new find makes you wonder - amethysts, emeralds, diamonds, shells - which do you love the most?  Don't despair.  Aldous Huxley's Mynah Bird sang the answer.
"Here and now Boys.  Here and Now."

Shells are for the Now.  This second.  Better than Heroin.  Instant gratification.  Found my way they cost less.

# CHAPTER XIV

# TRAYS

"For Christmas . . . oh my birthday . . . my birthday's coming soon, oh I don't have one single Wide Mouth Purpura. Oh I need it Mr. Richards. Please, please. Hey guys Mummy's writing a book. It isn't fair. Mummy has bad eyes. Please. Hmmmm . . . Isao . . . how about lending it to me? Just for my book? Just lending? Lending isn't bad. Please??"

Maybe because it's hard - that's why this game grows on you throughout the years. I have been playing it for 15 years at least one month out of twelve. If ever a house guest friend of mine finds something perfect, he hides it, knowing I'll be begging.

I remember once, during a storm, the air filled with crashing waves. I made the children chug slowly towards the Outside, our boat filling up with water at about the same time as their pleading,

"Mummy, you can't swim to shore, you'll drown."

"Mummy, you hate sharks. Sharks always bite in murky water."

I jumped overboard. I swam, lifted my head, breathed, swam again, almost drowned, crashing and rolling to the beach. I walked. Oh I walked miles. I looked. I searched. Now in This Storm something was going to happen. Yes sir, my two best white coral trees - oh perfect, perfect coral so delicate, so lacy white AND at the very end of the beach, a tiny brown glow. "Oh please God, oh Please." I dug a little. It couldn't be . . . it couldn't . . . I dug some more and an absolutely perfect, just dead, DIVINE Measled Cowrie. Hurrah! All shiny, spotted and perfect.

"Is he my favourite?", I often ask myself - as often as I regard my trays - trays being so satisfactory an answer for displaying shells if boats are small and lacking table tops.

A tray is easy to store. A tray is able to fit into almost any bureau drawer. On a tray you lay a thick, brilliant paper napkin - deepest red, forest green, lapis blue. What is your favourite colour? Good paper napkins are rich as damask. Their colour is your background. Through the years you can build upon this colour.

After 15 years of collecting, I have four trays. That's all. But what perfection of shouting beauty these four. One day I took them out to see what I could see, and have a little restoration of soul. Mark was 11 years old.

"Oh my gosh Mummy," he called excitedly to his mother, "come quick. What's that?"

"That's my shell tray."

"Oh my gosh Mummy, look at Aunt Cécile's Shell Tray. Oh Aunt Cécile, it's for a museum. Oh it's so beautiful. What's that?"

"That's an Angular Triton. Fiona found him when she was three years old."

Mark was so enthusiastic. His eyes gleamed.

"Oh could I get a tray like that?"

"Could you ever. Come, choose your paper napkin. I have a whole box of different colours to choose from."

"Let's begin right now. Oh please. Let's begin. I need a tray too. Come on guys. Let's go shelling. Could I have a red paper napkin? Could I Aunt Cécile?"

Carrier Shells - Did man ever make anything like these shells which paste other shells upon their conical backs, their shiny insides looking like frothy prune whip? Salud Mummy and Baby - oh impossible luck both on the same beach during a Full Moon Tide. What happened, oh what happened to cause you both to die together?

And you Mr. Orange Scallop. I remember you. Wild waves crashing over my head, three feet of water, something orange in all that murky tumbled sea. Not a perfect Pecten and orange? "Hey Pascal - hey look he's perfect!", I shouted as I grabbed him, hardly believing anything so lucky could be happening to me.

My first 1/2 inch baby Princess Helmet, so cunning, so teeny, so exquisite.

Pascal's leafy jewel box upon a silver Wing Oyster with glorious worms coiling around - the find of that year.

Fiona when she was three years old, blue eyes sparkling, blond hair dancing, hiding - hiding something behind her back something . . .

"Well you have to guess Mummy. Guess."

Humouring her, we were all of us guessing. What could three years old possibly find?

"It's something pretty special Mummy. You're going to like it a lot."

Oh I do Fiona. I do. MY ONLY DEAD PERFECT ANGULAR TRITON after 18 years of hunting. I love him. I have never found another dead one in all that time.

My first Natica canrena on that far away beach when the engine wouldn't start, and the sun was setting all forlorn. Wouldn't somebody come, please, wouldn't they?

In the beginning, your treasures exhilarate the spirit. As the years pass, however, profusion rears its ugly head. I always wonder, is it possible that few is best, is it possible that "profusion is confusion?"

With the Shell Game - if one of your rules is the same as mine - Perfection - you need have little worry about profusion in the beginning. Perfect colour, perfect lip, perfect shine, creature just died, seemingly within a day - that's hard - very, very hard to find.

It seems to me one needs luck, wits, guessing, more luck, persistence, patience, and finally, during storms, a certain amount of valour.

Then, later, while gazing at your trays you can remember everything - all your adventures. You find yourself crooning little songs. It's hard to tear yourself away.

- Oh you families of Spirula spirula with mother-of-pearl insides.
- Oh Crabbies holding Crabbie conversations. Mummies and Children and Cousins and Uncles and Aunties.
- Oh Sea Eggs stiff and bristly.
- Rooster-tail Conch no need to mention you - you steal the show.
- Twelve little Oysters all together - silvery inside, fringy outside - Welcome Newcomers found by Michiko!
- Curled up Chiton. Don't worry. I like you curled up. Nobody tied you to a board to die thirstily in the sun.
- Star Fishes, Orange Spondylus holding babies, Golden Cockles, Hawk-wings, Sunshells, brightness and light, sailing and dancing.

Shells take a bow. Your presence is required to sing praises to the Lord for in this our time you were created that all might fall down and worship the cunning of His Eye and the greatness of His Hand.

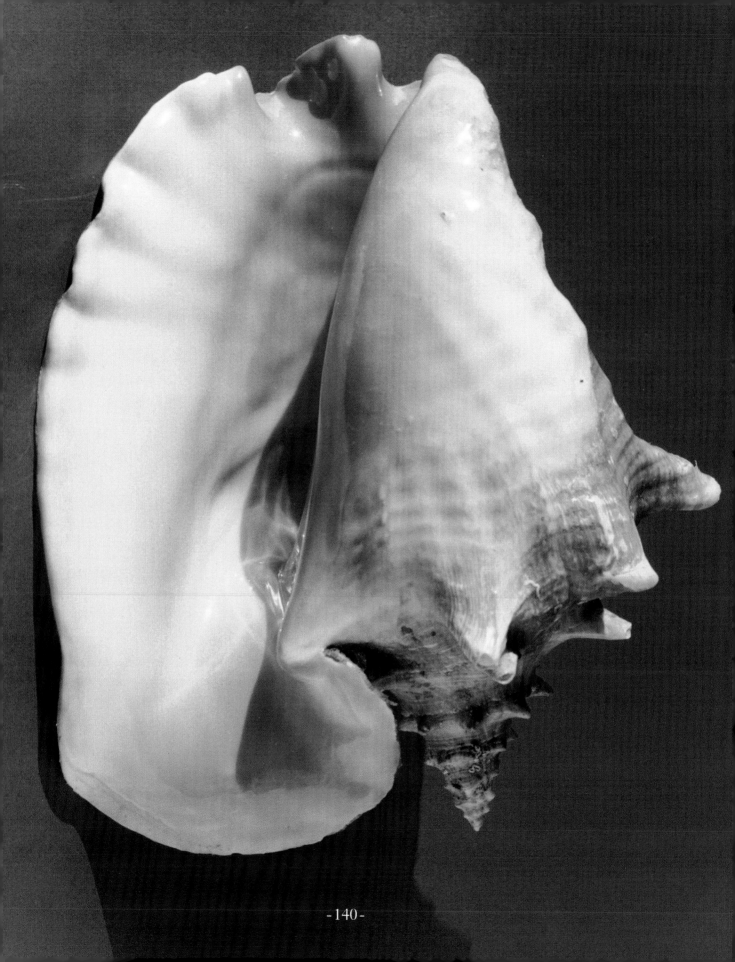

# CHAPTER XV

# THE QUEEN

I always know when a storm approaches, because home-made fishing boats come beating in at dusk of day to drop their anchors and spend the night. Long before the wind begins to howl, men climb into their rickety dinghies. Sometimes these dinghies seem as precarious as canoes. With powerful strokes of a single oar, one fisherman stands up sculling his boat towards mine. He brings chopped-up conch for salad; another brings nicely cleaned fish; a third brings shells.

"Oh yes ma'am, I does eat dese here. Dey's tasty."

I'm not accepting his shell present for my collection, because I have to <u>know</u> a shell was collected dead before adding it to the rest of my treasures. But for decoration on my boat, I love to add these strange shapes from other islands. I'm sure they eat them. Once, on a lonely atoll in the South Pacific, we found the remains of a fire with two charred Golden Cowries among the cinders.

Anyway, my fishermen come to trade - presents for supplies. They bring presents. I give them grits, flour, sugar,

"You gots some lard ma'am? We'se plain out of cookin' grease."

The generator boats banging the silence with their coughs and poundings, the Spanish Wells Scuba boats with their teams of merciless divers, the sleek, huge power boats . . . I greet overtures from these modernities with hooded, wary eyes and distant words.

But for my centuries old, earning-their-living-close-to-the-sea-and-God fishermen, I reserve a special warmth of welcome.

They come to the islands near our houseboats to chop dead wood. At night, I can see the flames of their little cooking fires on deck, dancing in the dusk. Fragrance of outdoor cooking eddies in the night air. They're shy; they're proud - these fishermen. They're the real Kings. They don't have radios. No engines for them. They look. They listen. They feel. And when I see their home-made sails tacking in at twilight, I say to myself,

"Hum . . . a storm is coming tomorrow."

Always I ask how many conchs they have this trip, and always the answer is in the thousands.

"Well ma'am, we done had some luck. Yesterday we does catch 700 of dese here conch."

As I write, three small boats, each with over 2,000 Conch, rock in the harbour waiting for dawn to light their way to Nassau.

They bring back memories of the Long Ago. In that Long Ago, before I invented this Shell Game, when its rules were just beginning to percolate through my mind, when I used Conch to catch fish, (Conch is very fine fish bait), I used to argue with myself:

> "Surely for the decoration of my boat I may kill one shell. Surely
> I may kill one Queen Conch a year. I will use the shell for Beauty,
> and the meat for fish bait. Isn't that fair?"

Then I would travel to places where Queen Conch lived in hoards. I would wander happily through eel grass, lifting up first one and then another. Sometimes this would take me a whole day. The colour I was searching had to be incredible. Deepest, wildest pink or orange for Queens radiant in full maturity. The lip had to be absolutely perfect. If I was going to kill, I wanted to kill carefully. Juveniles, not full grown, their lips not heavy and mature, but finely fluted and shiny as new porcelain, were also in their own way beauties worth considering. Sometimes their brilliant orange faded to a strange green line, an almost sunset green, which bordered their lips in a most compelling manner.

When finally I found a perfect specimen, I would wrap him in a heavy beach towel. Conchs have feet. They can move. If they are on a hard surface, they can tip themselves over with a crash, chipping their lips. However with my Conch wrapped up in his heavy towel, I never had any fears continuing my exploration - indulging my insatiable wanderlust. At each new beach I would unwrap my Conch and let him have a rest in six inches of water and pure sand where I could keep my eye on him if he went wandering. Finally home, I would wrap him up again - this time in layers of Saran Wrap, placing him face down within the Freezer.

> "Please conch, please die quickly," I would implore.

This was always my hardest moment. This was when Melancholy assailed my mind. It didn't matter how much I implored. Even when I didn't want to, I couldn't help remembering the prayers of a tough old man thrust naked into a deep freeze of hell day after day by Nazi "Scientists" experimenting with the effects of cold upon the human body. His pleas hurt me, etched as they were with horror into my brain. Mournfully, I suspected all my lovely Strombus gigas Linné 1758 used those same kinds of words as they went down into their unconsciousness. I could always hear that muscular foot thumping against the Saran Wrap - pleading with the March of Fate to stop marching,

> "All my luscious green algae, my babies, my companions of the
> heart, sunlight filtering through the glass of sea - Wait - you're
> making a horrible mistake. Wait . . ."

Once the final deed was done, once Strombus gigas Linné 1758 was finally frozen, and once I had somewhat recovered from this dreadful ordeal, usually several days later, I would put him very carefully into a bucket of salt water so he would not chip. In an hour or so when he was thawed, I would take his operculum, the horny brown end of his foot, and as much of his body as I could comfortably grasp with one hand. Gently, gently I would ease the whole creature out of the shell which I was holding with my other hand.

If I pulled fast, if I was a little hasty, or if the conch was not quite thawed out, a piece might be left behind. Dead conch left in the shell is one of the most loathsome smells in the world. I would be <u>very</u> careful.

Once he was out of his shell, (the animal itself), I would cut away his guts, and, after washing him thoroughly in the flowing tide, (conch meat is exceedingly slimy), I would put him into a baggie, refreezing it ready for my next fishing trip. The shell I would wrap in an old towel, putting it carefully upright in an empty plastic bucket to take to the beach when everybody was finally ready. Now I, and my conch, and a good stiff vegetable brush, and a good stiff toothbrush were ready for the fray.

I would wet and brush, wet and brush the green eely grass and algae from **THE OUTSIDE OF THE SHELL** with the vegetable brush. Then I would use the toothbrush to remove the muddy debris from in between its little brown lines.

At last I was finished. At last I was proud possessor of a decoration fit for any kingdom, clean, perfect, and without smell. He would fade. Eventually my beautiful Conch would fade, but not so fast as a bowl of roses.

I comforted myself that I had used the creature for bait, the house for beauty, and that my one a year compared not unfavorably with those 6,000 rocking in my harbour. I told myself Conch is part of the staple diet of the Bahamians. When they can afford it, it is as much a part of their staple diet as is wheat for the Canadians. I tried not to feel guilty, and I tried not to say, "I'm sorry" every time I passed the main attraction of my living room.

But sometimes I couldn't help thinking of those little eyes peering, that little head trustingly nibbling, searching for food. If I was really honest, I could use beef for bait. Fish love beef. So then each time my eye rested upon Madam Queen, I was confronted with compromise. I murdered her for her Beauty. It was awful. Arguments kept attacking me like hoards of bees. I never had any peace. I was always uneasy. My conscience was perpetually stricken. But if I played the game I was thinking of inventing, with no exceptions, I never <u>would</u> find a perfect Queen Conch. Never. I <u>liked</u> perfect Queen Conchs. I did. I needed them. How could I give them up? How could I sternly face never owning a perfect Queen Conch again?

One day, however, the year arrived when the cost of annual Queen Conchs for Celine skyrocketed out of control. Her Lust for Beauty lost. Her Shell Game won.

Suddenly she was free.  She found no replacements for her faded and dusty Queens - true - but at least she no longer had to endure that harassed, barbed wire probing of thorny oysters molesting her conscience.

"One - only one a year Celine."

"Bahamians eat thousands of Conch each week Celine."

"For heavens sake, Celine, some of the new land in the old harbour of Nassau is constructed entirely out of Conch Shells."

"If you eat beef you murder the cow Celine.  You don't need to eat beef."

"Lambs are frolicsome and cunning Celine.  Do you eat lamb? What about chickens, ducks, turkeys?"

"Let's move onto wheat Celine.  Please consider a field of golden wheat waving ripely below a blue Alberta sky.  Maybe wheat screams as it feels those heavy blades chopping.  Only we humans never learned wheat language so we can't <u>hear</u> the terror of death, we only <u>see</u> the tractor busily doing tractor business."

"All life is a compromise, Celine.  You grow the flower in your garden, but how do you like chopping it for a vase in your house? The chopping part you hate, the vase and the flower part inside your house you love."

"But I grew it for cutting."

"It dies anyway on its own stem almost as quickly as inside my vase of water."

"Today I killed a Hermit Crab."

"It's not as bad to kill Hermit Crabs as it is to kill shells."

"You just said killing is bad."

"Well, shells **MAKE** houses; Hermit Crabs only **BORROW** houses."

"It's not up to you to decide what's important to kill and what's not important.  You're not God.  Who are you to say, 'Murder Hermits; Save shells'?"

"Let's start again."

"Let's."

"You're going around and around in circles."

"Complicated things go round and round in circles."

"Shells."

"Yes, shells."

"To you shell animals are important animals to be treated with respect. They're sensitive to pain. After Full Moon nights, beaches always look as if shell revels have sirened the night so maybe they're sensitive to beauty. They know how to create some of the most beautiful colours and shapes in the universe."

"Yes."

"If we keep going in the Exumas for the next ten years the way we have been going for the last ten years one morning there will be no more shells."

"No more. That's right. Because even now for really vast populations of shells on beaches and in mangrove swamps, you have to go to dangerous, tricky areas where there are so many reefs most humans are scared, so most humans are absent."

"The more humans the fewer shells.
 The fewer humans the more shells."

"So if people played your game . . ."

"Yes, if they played my game, shells might come back again. People might have just as much fun. People like challenges. Most people have a hunting instinct to some degree or other."

"That's right. Most people **LIKE** Treasure Hunts."

"Yes."

"People might have even more fun."

"They might, especially now they've read my book. They might feel sick when they're hanging their poor little creature with a pin or boiling him on the stove. Now they know what they're doing they might mind."

"But this way, if they're clever, they could have the shell without the killing."

"That's right."

"Their shell would be free."

"The price tag for Beauty wouldn't have to hurt anyone."

"No one's Death need mutilate anyone's Conscience."

"If you feel this way about Shells, what about People?"

"The trick is to begin.   You have to begin somewhere.  This Shell Game is a beginning.  Each person who plays it, after awhile, can't help feeling a new kind of Reverence for Life."

"Celine you're crazy."

"It's about that bell."

"What bell?"

"The bell that keeps on tolling."

"You mean . . . 'never send to know for whom the bell tolls . . .'?"

" Yes.  It bothered John Donne too."

**De Wisdom**

# DEFINITIONS

Shells are either a single spiral shell called a **UNIVALVE**, or else they are two halves, "whose matching sides are hinged together" called a **BIVALVE**. Sometimes you find only half of a bivalve, because the other half has been washed away or ripped apart by the waves before it reaches the beach.

*Florida's Fabulous Seashells*
Page 2

**APERTURE** – a large opening in a shell from which the head protrudes, and, on occasion, a lot of the body.

**FOOT** – as in the Queen Conch, where the body extends itself from the aperture in order to propel itself along the seabed.

**OPERCULUM** – When present, a horny or hard, shelly structure is attached to the foot. The ones I have seen are brown. Either they can be used as trap doors to snap shut the creature inside, and seal him up tight from roving marauders, or they can be used as aids to propulsion along the seabed floor. Watch a Queen Conch moving. Then pick it up. Instantly you will recognize its operculum.

**PERIOSTRACUM** – an outside covering of many shells. It can be "thin, thick, smooth, rough, or hairy."

*Seashells of North America*
Page 51

**VENTRAL** – The underside of a shell. The shiny side of Helmets or Conchs.

**DORSAL** – The top side of a shell. The back side or the rough outside of a shell.

**RADULA** – are teeth attached to a ribbon in the mouth. Sometimes they are used as a rasp and once in awhile as a stinger. All Molluscs except for bivalves have them.

*Seashells of North America*
Page 25

**TEST** – Dead Sand Dollars, or Sea Eggs, or Sea Urchins are not actually called shells. Their skeletons, when denuded, no longer having those long sharp spines attached, are called Tests.

**Rams Horns**
**Spirula spirula**
**Linné, 1758**
**1/2"- 1"**

**Barnacle Limpet**
**Lottia balanoides**
**Reeve, 1855**
**1/4"- 1/2"**

**Green Keyhole Limpet**
**Diodora viridula**
**Lamarck, 1822**
**3/4"- 1"**

**Common Dove Shell**
**Columbella mercatoria**
**Linné, 1758**
**1/2"- 3/4"**

**Emerald Nerite**
**Smaragdia viridis**
**viridemaris**
**Maury, 1917**
**1/4"- 1/3"**

These are
faded. They
should be
bright pink
with four
teeny spots

**Four-spotted Trivia**
**Trivia quadripunctata**
**Gray, 1827 1/4"**

**Coffee Bean Trivia**
**Trivia pediculus**
**Linné, 1758 1/2" or less**

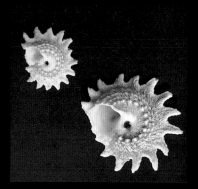

**Long-spined Star Shell
with baby
Astraea phoebia
Röding, 1798
2"- 3 1/2"**

**Dorsal view
Long-spined Star Shell**

**Kitten's Paw
Plicatula gibbosa
Lamarck, 1801
about 1" or less**

**'Coon Oyster
Ostrea frons
Linné, 1758
1"- 2 1/2"**

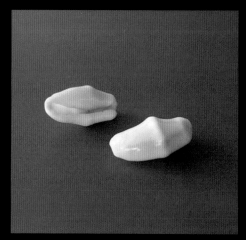

**Flamingo Tongue
Cyphoma gibbosum
Linné, 1758 3/4"- 1"**

**Bleeding Tooth
Nerita peloronta
Linné, 1758 1"- 1 1/3"**

**Gaudy Asaphis**
**Asaphis deflorata**
**Linné, 1758**
**1 1/2"- 2 1/2"**

**Atlantic Hairy Triton**
**Cymatium pileare martinianum**
**Orbigay, 1842**
**2"- 6"**

**Ventral view**
**Atlantic Hairy Triton**

**False Cup and Saucer**
**Cheilea equestris**
**Linné, 1758**
**3/4" - 1 1/4"**

**Smooth Scotch Bonnet**
**Phalium cicatricosum**
**Gmelin, 1791**
**1" - 2 1/2"**

**"With a single**
**row of small pustules**
**on the shoulder**
**of each whorl"**
**p. 118 Humfrey**

**Knobby Triton Cymatium muricinum**
**Röding, 1798, 1"- 2"**

**Smooth Scotch Bonnet**
**another form of the above**

**Princess Venus Clam**
**Antigona listeri**
**Gray, 1838**
**2"- 4"**

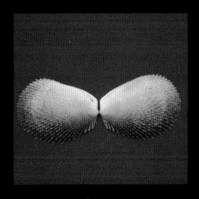

**Rough Lima**
**Lima scabra**
**Born, 1778**
**1"- 3"**

**Great Tellin**
**Tellina magna**
**Spangler, 1798**
**3"- 4 1/2"**

**Reticulated Cowrie Helmet**
**Cypraecassis testiculus**
**Linné, 1758**
**1" -3"**

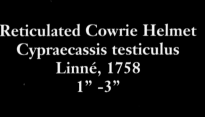

**Measled Cowrie**
**Mature Specimen**
**Cypraea zebra**
**Linné, 1758**
**1 1/4"- 4"**

**Measled Cowrie**
**vental view**
**mature specimen**

**Atlantic Yellow Cowrie**
**Cypraea spurca acicularis**
**Gmelin, 1791**
**1/2"- 1 1/4"**

**Measled Cowrie**
**advanced teenager immature shell no spots**
**Cypraea zebra**
**Linné, 1758**
**1 1/4"- 4"**

**Angular Triton**
**Cymatium femorale**
**Linné, 1758**
**3"- 7"**

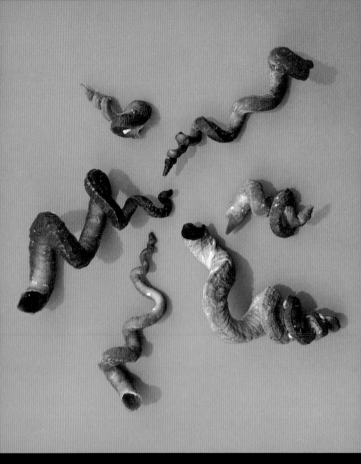

**West Indian Worm Shell**
**Vermicularia spirata**
**Philippi, 1836**
**up to 4"**

## Scaly Wing Oyster
### Pteria longisquamòsa
### Dunker, 1852

## Calcareous Green Algae
### Udotea flabellum
### Ellis & Solandex, 1786

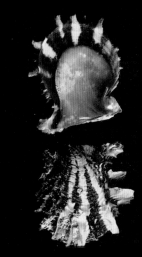

## Atlantic Pearl Oyster
### Pinctada radiata
### Leach, 1814 1"- 4"

**Another colour form species figured at top.**

**Same middle left**

**Queen Conch**
**Strombus gigas**
**Linné, 1758**
**Baby 1"-2"**
**Teenager 3"- 4"**
**Adult 5"- 12"**
**See opercula p. 185**

**Rooster-tail Conch**
**Strombus gallus**
**Linné, 1758**
**4"- 6 1/2"**

**Milk Conch**
**Young Specimens**
**Strombus costatus**
**Gmelin, 1791**
**4"- 7"**

**Milk Conch**
**a little older than top right**

**Rooster- tail Conch**
**Ventral view**

**Hawk-wing Conch**
**Strombus raninus**
**Gmelin, 1791 2"- 4"**

**Hawk-wing Conch**
**Dorsal view**

**King Helmet**
**Cassis tuberosa**
**Linné, 1758**
**fully mature 4"- 10"**

**King Helmet**
**Dorsal view**

King Helmet
Younger Version
Cassis tuberosa
Linné, 1758
4"- 10"

King Helmet
Younger Version
Ventral view

Flame Helmet
Dorsal and Ventral views
also called
Princess Helmet
Cassis flammea
Linné, 1758
3"- 5"

**West Indian Chank**
**Turbinella angulata**
**Lightfoot, 1786**
**7"- 14"**

**Apple Murex**
**Dorsal and Ventral views**
**Murex pomum**
**Gmelin, 1791**
**2"- 4 1/2"**

**Atlantic Grey Cowrie**
**Juveniles**
**Orange Yellow Variety**
**Cypraea cinerea**
**Gemelin, 1791**
**3/4"- 1 1/2"**

**Queen Conch**
**old lady with coral**
**on her back**
**Strombus gigas**
**Linné, 1758**
**5"- 8"**

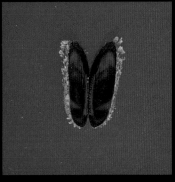

**Red-brown Ark**
**Barbatia cancellaria**
**Lamarck, 1819**
**1"- 1 1/2"**

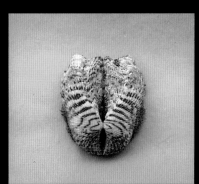

**Turkey Wing**
**Arca zebra**
**Swainson, 1883**
**2"- 3"**

**Tulip Mussel**
**Modiolus americanus**
**Leach, 1815**
**1"- 4"**

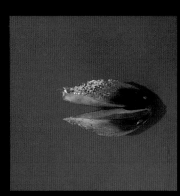

**Tulip Mussel**

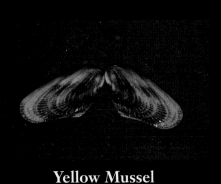

**Yellow Mussel**
**Brachidontes citrinus**
**Röding, 1798, 1"- 1 1/2"**

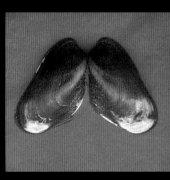

**Tulip Mussel**
**same as centre 2 pictures (cleaned)**

**Gaudy Asaphis
Asaphis deflorata
Linné, 1758
1 1/2"- 2 1/2"**

**Cross-barred Venus Clam
Chione cancellata
Linné, 1767
1"- 1 3/4"**

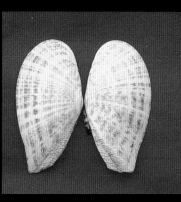

**Speckled Tellin
Tellina listeri
Röding, 1798
2"- 3 1/2"**

**Speckled Tellin
Ventral view**

**Nucleus Scallop
Argopecten nucleus
Born, 1778
1"- 2"**

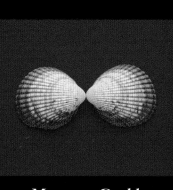

**Magnum Cockle
Trachycardium magnum
Linné, 1758**

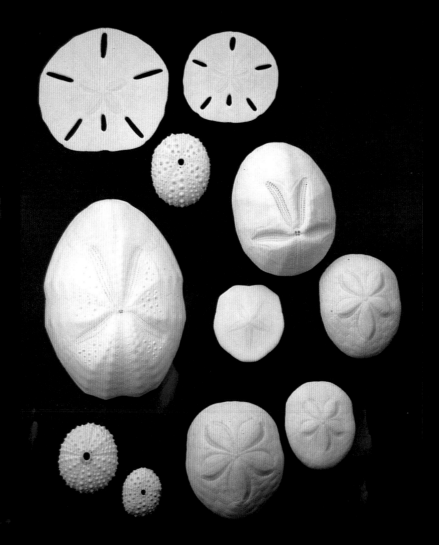

**3 Bottom Right**
**Sea Biscuit**
**Clypeaster rosacea**
**Linné, 1758**

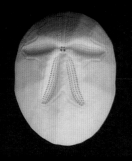

**Heart Urchin**
**Brissus unicolor**
**Leske, 1778**

**Sea Egg**
**Sea Urchin**
**Lytechinus variegatus**
**Lamarck, 1816**

**Sea Pancake**
**Laganum species**

**Sea egg**
**Sea Urchin (denuded)**
**Echinometra lucunter**
**Linné, 1758**

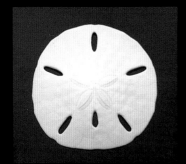

**Sand Dollar**

**Six-hole Keyhole Urchin**
**Leodia sexiesperforata**
**Leske, 1778**

**Heart Urchin**
**Plagiobrissus grandis**
**Gmelin, 1791**

**Crown Cone**
**Conus regius**
**Gmelin, 1791**
**2"- 3"**

**Mouse Cone**
**Conus mus**
**Hwass, 1792**
**1"- 1 1/2"**

**True Tulip**
**Fasciolaria tulipa**
**Linné, 1758**
**3"- 10"**

**Warty Cone**
**Conus verrucosus Hwass**
**also called Jasper Cone Conus jaspideus**
**Gmelin, 1791**
**1/2"- 1"**

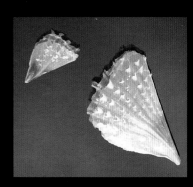

**Spiny Pen Shell**
**Atrina seminuda Lamarck, 1819**
**5"- 9" see p. 204**
**for Amber Pen Shell**

172

## Aequipecten muscosus Wood, 1828

**Goldmouth
Hairy Triton
Cymatium nicobaricum
Röding, 1798
1"- 2 1/2"**

**Deltoid Rock Shell
Thais deltoidea
Lamarck, 1822
1"- 2"**

**Atlantic Bubble Shell
Bulla striata
Bruguière, 1792
1"- 1 1/2"**

**True Tulip**
**Fasciolaria tulipa**
**Linné, 1758**
**3"- 10"**

**Atlantic Partridge Tun**
**Tonna maculosa**
**Dillwyn, 1817**
**2" - 5"**

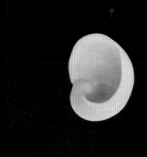

**Common Baby's Ear**
**Sinum perspectivum**
**Say, 1831**
**1" - 1 1/2"**

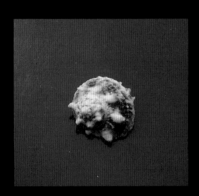

**Chestnut Turban**
**Turbo castaneus**
**Gmelin, 1791 3/4"- 1 1/2"**

**True Tulip**
**another colour variety**
**Fasciolaria tulipa**
**Linné, 1758**
**3'- 10"**

**Wide mouth Purpura**
**Purpura patula**
**Linné, 1758**
**2" - 3 1/2"**

**West Indian Worm Shell**
**Vermicularia spirata Philippi, 1836**
**up to 4"**

**Purple Sea Fan**
**attached to a stick with some coral**

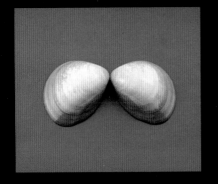

**Common Egg Cockle**
**Laevicardium laevigatum**
**Linné, 1758**
**1"- 2"**

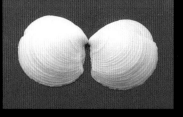

**Pennsylvania Lucina
cleaned
Lucina pensylvanica
Lynné, 1758
1"- 2"**

**Same not cleaned**

**Red Jewel Box
Chama sarda
Reeve, 1847 3/4"- 1"
outside of shell is smooth**

**Acropagia fausta**

**Faust Tellin
Tellina fausta
Pulteney
3"**

**Leafy Jewel Box (yellow)
Chama macerophylla
Gmelin, 1791**

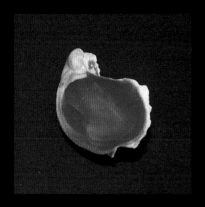

**Cross-barred
Venus Clam
Chione cancellata
Linné, 1767
fresher and
sharper than p.169**

**Red Jewel Box
see centre
opposite page**

**Leafy Jewel Box
on an Atlantic Winged
Oyster
Chama macerophylla
Gmelin, 1791
1"-3"**

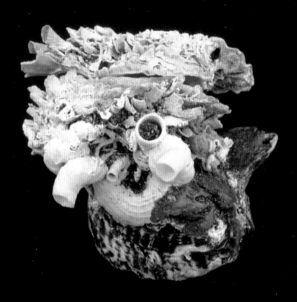

**Leafy Jewel Box
same name as centre**

**King Venus Clam
Chione paphia
Linné, 1767
1"- 1 1/2"**

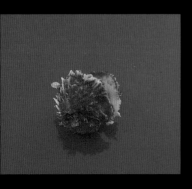

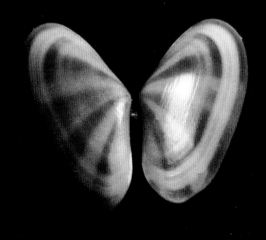

**Sunshell or Sunrise Tellin**
Tellina radiata

**Sunshell or Sunrise Tellin**
**Tellina radiata unimaculata**
**Lamarck,**
**2"- 4"**
**no sun rays, just horizontal bands,**
**only found by this author on outside beaches**

**Sunshell or Sunrise Tellin**
**Tellina radiata**
**Linné, 1758**
**2"- 4"**

**Triton's Trumpet**
**Charonia variegata Lamarck, 1816**
**10"- 18" See bottom right**

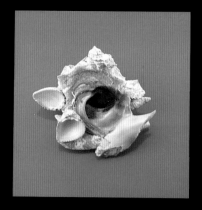

**Atlantic Carrier Shell**
**Xenophxa conchyliophra**
**2"- 2 1/2" Born, 1780**
**see bottom left**

**Zigzag Scallop**
**Pecten ziczac Linné, 1758**
**2"- 4"**
**Top only- bottom is**
**curved like a saucer**

**'Coon Oyster**
**Ostrea frons Linné, 1758**
**1"- 2 1/2"**

**Alantic Carrier Shell**
**Born, 1780**

**Triton's Trumpet**

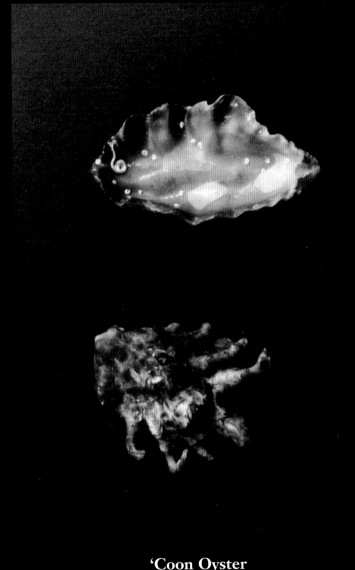

**'Coon Oyster**
**Ostrea frons**
**Linné, 1758**
**1"- 2 1/2"**

**Sea Egg or Sea Urchin**
**Eucidaris tribuloides**
**Lamarck, 1816**
**Up to 2 1/4"**

**Lucky Bean
(small)
Thick banded
Sea Bean
Macuna urens
1"- 1 1/2"**

**Lucky Bean (large)
Sea Heart
Intada scandeus  1 1/2"- 2 1/2"**

**Opercula
Horny foot or door
of Queen Conch
Strombus gigas
Linné, 1758
Bottom one from a True
Tulip**

**Sea Egg or
Sea
Urchin
Test
1"- 2"**

**Arbacia punctulata
Lamarck, 1816**

**Chestnut Latirus
Leucozonia nassa
Gmelin, 1791
1 1/2"- 2"**

**Florida Worm Shell**
**Petaloconchus floridamus**
**Olsson & Hanbison, 1953**
**irregularly coiled and**
**attached to some object**
**along the whole length**
**of one side**
**Humfrey p. 83**

**Netted Olive**
**Oliva reticularis**
**Lamarck, 1811**
**many colour varieties**
**including white**

**Colourful Atlantic Natica**
**Natica canrena**
**Linné, 1758**
**1"- 2"**

**Fastigiella carinata**
**Reeve, 1848**

**Ivory Cerith**
**Cerithium eburneum Bruquière, 1792**
**3/4" - 1"**

**Long-spined Sea Urchin**
**Diadema antillarum**
**Philippi, 1845**

**Rough Girdle Chiton**
**Ceratozona squalida**
**C.B. Adams, 1845**

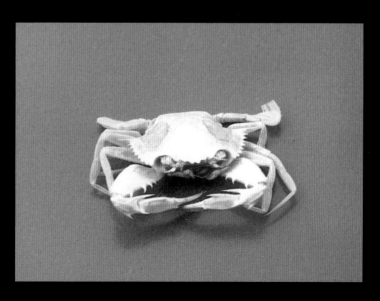

**Swimming Crab**
**Portunus species**

**1/2 an Ornate Scallop**
**Chlamys ornata**
**Lamarck, 1819**
**1"- 1 !/2"**

**Atlantic Bittersweet**
**open same as left**

**Atlantic Bittersweet**
**Glycymeris undata**
**Linné, 1758**
**about 2"**

**Decussate Bittersweet**
**Glycymeris decussata**
**Linné, 1758**
**about 2"**

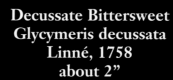

**Papyridea simisulcata**
**Gray, 1825**
**1/2"**

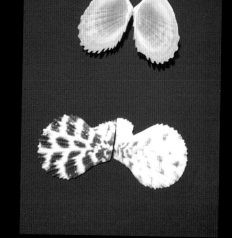

**Ornate Scallop**
**Chlamys ornata**
**Lamarck, 1819**
**1"- 1 1/2"**

**Test or Case of denuded Sea**
**Egg or Sea Urchin**
**Eucidaris tribuloides**
**Lamarck, 1816**

**Tesellated Nerite**
**Nerita tessellata**
**Gmelin, 1791**
**1/2"- 3/4"**

**Livid Natica**
**Natica livida**
**Pfeiffer, 1840**
**1/4"- 1/2"**

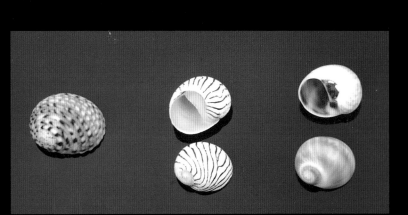

**McGinty's Latirus**
**Latirus mcgintyi**
**Pilsbry 1 1/2"- 2 1/2"**

**Short Tailed Latirus**
**Latirus angulatus**
**Röding, 1798**

**Knobby Triton**
**Cymatium muricinum**
**Röding, 1798**
**1" - 2"**

**White or Variable Nassa**
**Nassarius albus**
**Say, 1826**
**1/2"**

**White Spotted Marginella**
**Prunum guttatum**
**Dillwyn, 1817**
**1/2" - 3/4"**

**White Spotted Marginella**
**in various stages of growth**

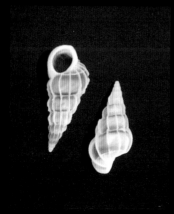

**Lamellose Wentletrap**
**Epitonium lamellosum**
**Lamarck, 1822**
**1"- 1 1/4"**

**Cancellate Cyclostreme**
**Cyclostrema cancellatum**
**Marryat, 1818**
**1/2"**

190

**Common Dove Shell**
**Columbella mercatoria**
**Linné, 1758**
**1/2" - 2/4"**

**Smooth Atlantic Tegula**
**Tegula fasciata**
**Born, 1778**
**1/2"- 3/4"**

**Atlantic Woodhouse**
**Morum oniscus**
**Linné, 1767**
**3/4"- 1"**

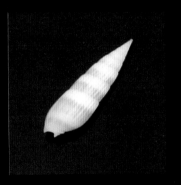

**Shiny Auger**
**Impages hastata**
**Gmelin, 1791**

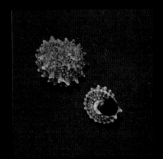

**(Top) False Prickly - Winkle**
**Echininus nodulosus**
**Pfeiffer, 1839**
**1/2"- 1"**

**Krebs Wentletrap**
**Epitonium krebsii**
**Mörch, 1874**

191

**Florida Jewel Box**
**Chama florida**
**Lamarck, 1819**
**about 1"**

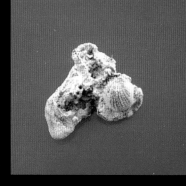

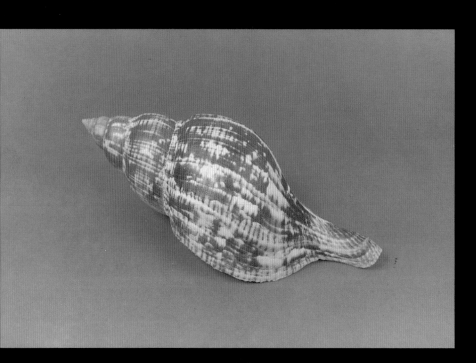

**True Tulip**
**Another color variation, p. 174**
**Fasciolaria tulipa**
**Linné, 1758**
**3"-10"**

**Angulate Periwinkle**
**Littorina angulifera**
**Lamarck, 1822**
**1"- 1 1/2"**
**considerably magnified**

**Rice Olivella**
**Rice Shell**
**Olivella floralia Duclos, 1853**
**1/2"**

**Barbados Mitre**
**Mitra barbadensis**
**Gmelin, 1791**
**1"- 2"**

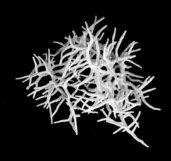

**Stinging Coral
Millepora alcicornis
Blainville, 1830**

**Beaded Sea Star
Astropecten articulatus
Say, 1825**

**Four Spotted Trivia
Trivia quadripunctata
Gray, 1827
about 1/4"
These are tiny and bright pink
19 to 24 riblets cross the outer lip.
A 1/2 Atlantic Thorny Oyster is holding them**

**Stinging Coral
Millepora alcicornis
Blainville, 1830**

**Sand dollar
Six-hole Keyhole
Urchin
Leodia sexiesperforata
Leske, 1778**

**Swimming Crab
Portunus species**

**Stinging coral**
**Millepora species**

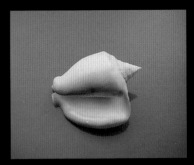

**Milk Conch**
**Strombus costatus**
**Gmelin, 1791**
**4"- 7" adult**

**Swimming Crab**
**Callinectes species**

**Purse Crab**
**Persephona species**

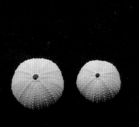

**Sea Egg**
**Tripneustes ventricosus**
**Lamarck, 1816**

**Stinging Coral**
**Millepota alcicornis**
**Blainville, 1830**

195

**Glossy Dove Shell**

**Glossy Dove Shell**
**Nitidella nitida**
**Lamarck, 1822**
**about 1/2" Blow up**

**Snowy Dwarf Olive**
**Olivella nivea**
**Gmelin, 1791**
**1/2"- 1"**

**Bottom Row**

**(left) Wobbly Keyhole Limpet Fissurella fascicularis Lamarck, 1822 3/4" - 1 1/4"**

**(centre) Cancellate Fleshy Limpet Lucapina suffusa Reeve, 1850 1"- 1 1/2"**

**(right) Green Keyhole Limpet Diodora viridula Lamarck, 1822 3/4"- 1"**

**Top row**

**(left) Knobby Keyhole Limpet Fissurella nodosa Born, 1778 1"- 1 1/2"**

**(centre) Lister's Keyhole Limpet Diodora listeri Orbigay, 1853 1 1/2"- 2"**

**(right) Barbados Key hole Limpet Fissurella barbadensis Gmelin, 1791 1" - 1 3/4"**

**Wobbly Keyhole Limpet Fissurella fascicularis Lamarck, 1822 3/4" - 1 1/4"**

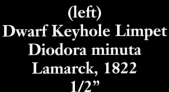

**(left) Dwarf Keyhole Limpet Diodora minuta Lamarck, 1822 1/2"**

**Cancellate Fleshy Limpet Lucapina suffusa Reeve, 1850 1" - 1 1/2"**

**Top left Eight Ribbed Limpet Hemitoma octoradiata Gmelin, 1791 1"**

**Emarginate Limpet Hemitoma emarginata Blainville, 1825 3/4" - 1 1/4"**

**Lister's Keyhole Limpet Diodora listeri Orbigny, 1853**

197

**Tiger Lucina**
**Codakia orbicularis**
**Linné, 1758**
**1"- 2 1/2"**
**(This is a baby. p. 61 shows one-**
**half an adult holding other babies.)**

**Gaudy Asaphis**
**Asaphis deflorata**
**Linné, 1758**
**1/2"- 2 1/2"**

**A Land Snail**
**Hemitrochus varians**
**Menke, 1829**

**Top Left Shell**
**Mossy Ark**
*Arca imbricata*
**Bruguière, 1789**
**1"- 1 1/2"**

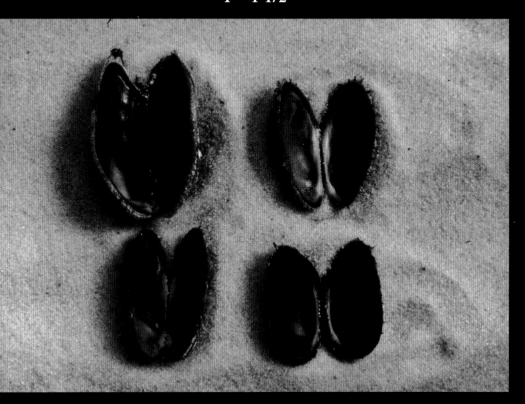

**Red-brown Ark**
*Barbatia cancellaria*
**Lamarck, 1819**
**1"- 1 1/2"**

**Milk Conch**
**Teenager-Ventral view**
**Sometimes Bright Purple**
*Strombus costatus*
**Gmelin, 1791**

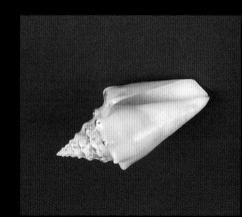

**Emperor Helmet
Ventral view
(note the rounded bottom
corners of the face)**

**King Helmet
Dorsal view**

**King Helmet
Cassis tuberosa
Linné, 1758
(note the triangular bottom corners)**

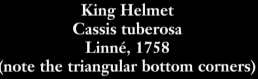

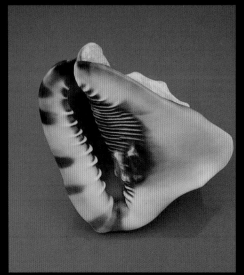

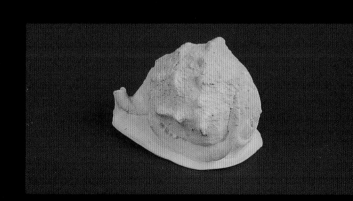

**Emperor Helmet
Cassis madagascariensis
Lamarck, 1822
Dorsal view**

**Colourful Atlantic Natica**
**Natica canrena**
**Linné, 1758**
**1"- 2"**

**Knorr's worm shell**
**Vermicularia knorri**
**Deshayes, 1843**
**up to 4"**

**Riise'sWorm shells**
**Serpulorbis riisei**
**Mörch, 1862**
**1 1/2"- 2"**

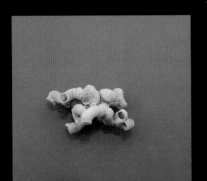

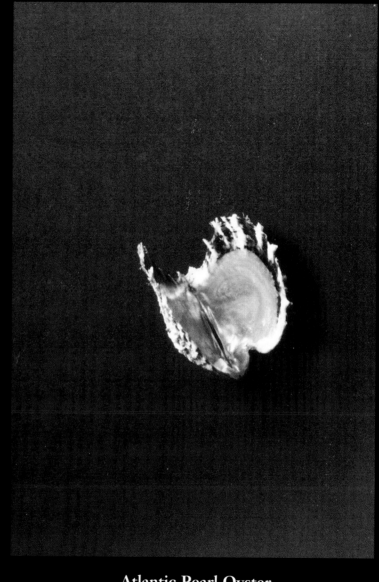

**Atlantic Pearl Oyster**
**Pinctada radiata**
**Leach, 1814**
**1"- 4"**

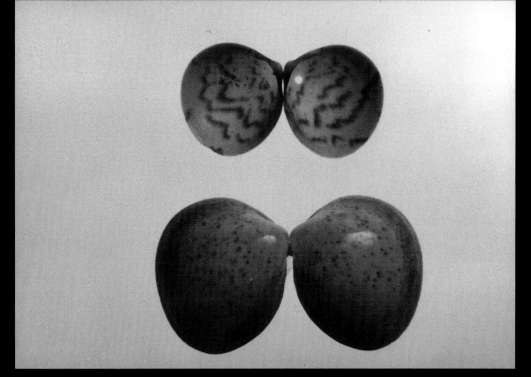

**Morton's Egg Cockle**
**Laevicardium mortoni**
**Conrad, 1830**

**King Helmet (baby)**
**Cassis tuberosa**
**Linné, 1758**
The back of this baby is cross
hatched with tiny fine lines

**Calcareous Green Algae**
**Penicillus capitatus**
**Lamarck, 1816**

**Amber Pen Shell**
**Pinna carnea**
**Gmelin, 1791**
**4"- 11"**
**See page 172 for other type**

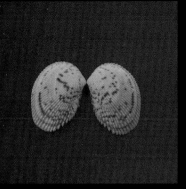

**Spiny Paper Cockle**
**Papyridea soleniformis**
**Bruguière, 1789**
**1"- 1 3/4"**

**(Left) Sunrise Tellin**
**another form**
**yellowish white**
**with red umbones**
**Tellina radiata**
**unimaculata**
**Lamarck,**
**2"- 4"**

**(Right) Rose Petal Tellin**
**Tellina lineata**
**Turton, 1819**
**1" - 1 1/2"**

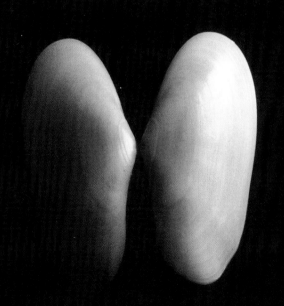

**Sunrise Tellin or Sunshell**
**Tellina radiata**

**West Indian Top Shell**
**Cittarium pica**
**Linné, 1758**

**Rooster-tail Conch**
**Strombus gallus**
**Linné, 1758**
**4"- 6 1/2"**

**Sunshell or Sunrise Tellin**
**Tellina radiata unimaculata**
**Lamarck,**
**2"- 4"**

**No sun rays - just horizontal bands**
**- only found by this author on outside beaches**

**Atlantic Carrier Shells**
**Xenophora conchyliophora**
**Born, 1780**
**2"- 2 1/2"**

**Giant Bahama Starfish**
**Oreaster reticulatus**

for

**PASCAL**

who supported and comforted,
guarded and encouraged me,
year after year after year




for

**MARY BAKER MOULDING**

who gave me permission to copy
her photographic layout identification




and finally for

**MARA**

who kept on saying,
"You'll make it Mummy.  One day
you'll be a Writer."

## TWO DESCRIPTIONS OF BABY SHELLS CLOCKWISE
Each Mummy Shell is half of an Atlantic Thorny Oyster - P.87
Spondylus americanus Hermann 1781, short spined variety, 3"-6"

McGinty's Latirus 2 of them
    Latirus mcgintyi Pilsbury 1 1/2"-2 2/1"
Gaudy Asaphis 2 closed ones together
    Asaphis deflorata Linné 1758, 1 1/2"-2 1/2"
Smooth Atlantic Tegula
    Tegula fasciata Born 1778, 1/2"-3/4"
Bottom Shell Baby Atlantic Hairy Triton
    Cymatium pileare martinianum Orbigny 1842, 2"-6"
Knorr's Worm Shell
    Vermicularia knorri Deshayes 1843, up to 4"
Rams Horn
    Spirula spirula Linné 1758, 1/2"-1"

## ANOTHER DESCRIPTION P.152
Same type of Mummy Shell as P.87 above
Baby Sea Egg or Denuded Sea Urchin
    Arbacia punctulata
Baby Sand Dollar
    Mellita perforata 1/2"-4"
Wobbly Keyhole Limpet
    Fissurella fascicularis Lamarck 1922, 3/4"-1 1/4"
Green Keyhole Limpet
    Diodora viridula Lamarck 1822, 3/4"-1"
Tessellated Nerite
    Nerita tessellata Gmelin 1791, 1/2"-3/4"
Gaudy Asaphis Purple
    Asaphis deflorata Linné 1758, 1 1/2"-2 1/2"
Common Dove Shell
    Columbella mercatoria Linné 1758,  1/2"-3/4"
Gaudy Asaphis Orange
    Asaphis deflorata Linné 1758, 1 1/2"-2 1/2"
White Spotted Marginella
    Prunum guttatum Dillwyn 1817, 1/2"-3/4"
Livid Natica
    Natica livida Pleiffer 1840, 1/2"
Smooth Atlantic Tegula
    Tegula fasciata Born 1778, 1/2"-3/4" (3 of them all close together)
West Indian Worm Shell
    Vermicularia spirata Philippi 1836, this one about 1"
 Dove Shell
    Nitidella nitida Lamarck 1822, 1/2"
In the center there is part of a True Tulip Shell showing
    Fasciolaria tulipa Linné 1758, 3"-5" this baby is 1"

# BIBLIOGRAPHY

Abbott, R. Tucker, 1985. *Seashells of the World*, 160 pp., illustrated by George and Marita Sandström, Golden Press, New York, N.Y., U.S.A.

Abbott, R. Tucker, 1968. *Seashells of North America*, 280 pp., 850 illustrations by George F. Sandström, Golden Press, New York, N.Y., U.S.A.

Abbott, R. Tucker, 1972. *King of the Seashell*, 256 pp., over 250 illustrations, Crown Publishers Inc., New York, N.Y., U.S.A.

Abbott, R. Tucker, 1984. *Collectible Shells of Southeastern U.S., Bahamas & Caribbean*, 64 pp., American Malacologists, Inc., Melbourne, Florida, U.S.A.

Abbott, R. Tucker and Dance, S. Peter, 1982. *Compendium of Seashells*, 410 pp., thousands of incredible colour illustrations, E. P. Dutton, New York, N.Y., U.S.A.

Abbott, R. Tucker and Stix, Hugh & Marguerite, 1968? *The Shell*, 188 pp., 82 hand tipped plates, Harry N. Abrams Inc., New York, N.Y., U.S.A. What a book. In my opinion, these are the best photographs that have ever been taken of any shells anywhere. This book is not for shell lovers. This book is for Treasure lovers. It is very expensive. It is very worth it. If a paperback is available it used to cost $29.95.

Bohlke, James E. and Chaplin, Charles C. G. 1968. *Fishes of the Bahamas*, 771 pp., hundreds of superb photographs, 36 color plates, Livingston Publishing Company, Wynnewood, Pa., U.S.A.

Burgess, C. M., 1970. *The Living Cowries*, 389 pp., the most superb photographs, Joint Publication A. S. Barnes & Carlton Beal, Cranbery, N.J., U.S.A. One of The All Time Great Shell Books ever put together anywhere. No world voyaging Yacht should be without a copy.

Coleman Neville, 1975. *What Shell is That?*, 308 pp., unbelievable photographs, Paul Hamlyn Pty Ltd., Dee Why West, N.S.W., Australia.

Dance, S. Peter, 1972. *Shells and Shell Collecting*, 128 pp., 110 photographs, Hamlyn Publishing Group Ltd., Feltham, Middlesex, England.

Dance, S. Peter, 1974. *The Collector's Encyclopedia of Shells*, 270 pp., hundreds of excellent photographs, McGraw Hill Book Co., Great Britain.

Emerson, William K., 1972.. *Shells*, 295 pp., photographer Andreas Feininger, hundreds of gorgeous photographs, The Viking Press Inc., New York, N.Y., U.S.A.

Fields, Meredith H., Editor, 1987. *1988 Yachtsman's Guide to the Bahamas*, 418 pp., Tropic Isle Publishers, Inc., Red Bank, N.J., U.S.A.

Humfrey, Michael, 1975. *Sea Shells of the West Indies*, 351 pp., 32 plates, HarperCollins Publishing Ltd., London, England. This is a fabulous book by a policeman with all the identification for shells that any beginner in the West Indies or the Exumas might desire.

Morris, Percy A., 1973, *A Field Guide to Shells of the Atlantic*, 329 pp., 76 plates, Houghton Mifflin Co.,Boston,Mass.,U.S.A. Edited by William J. Clench.

Moulding, Mary Baker, 1967. *Shells at our Feet*, 102 pp., photographs by the author, Sea Scapers, Winnetka, Illinois, U.S.A.

Popov,N.&D,1991. *Island Expedition*. Brilliant photographers of the Exuma Cays, the Popovs have kindly lent me the masterpiece which appears on p.11.

Rigg, J. Linton, 1949. *Bahama Islands*, 197 pp., 29 illustrations, 53 charts, D. Van Nostrand Co., Inc., Princeton, N.J., U.S.A.

Sabelli, Bruno, 1980. *Guide to Shells*, 512 pp., Feinberg, Harold S., Editor, Simon & Schuster, N.Y., N.Y, U.S.A.

Stix, Hugh & Marguerite and Abbott, R. Tucker, 1968? *The Shell*, 188 pp., 82 hand tipped plates, Harry N. Abrams Inc., New York, N.Y., U.S.A. What a book. In my opinion, these are the best photographs that have ever been taken of any shells anywhere. This book is not for shell lovers. This book is for Treasure lovers. It is very expensive. It is very worth it. If a paperback is available it used to cost $4.95.

Villas, C. N. and N. R., 1970. *Florida Marine Shells*, 170 pp., 14 plates, Charles E. Tuttle Co., Tokyo, Japan.

Voss, Gilbert L., 1976. *Seashore Life of Florida and the Caribbean*, 168 pp., 280 clear drawings and 19 full colour photographs. E.A. Seaman Publishing, Inc., Miami, Florida, U.S.A.

Weaver, Clifton S., and du Pont, John E., 1970. *The Living Volutes*, 375 pp., photographs to die over, Delaware Museum of Natural History, Greenville, U.S.A.

Williams, Winston, 1988. *Florida's Fabulous Seashells and Seashore Life*, 112 pp. Photographer Pete Carmichael. The best shell paperback I have ever seen with unbelievable photographs. World Publications, Tampa, Florida, U.S.A.

Book which sank to the bottom of the Sea re. p.15. This was a sad happening in 1979. I hope its author will forgive me for quoting without permission.

# PHOTOGRAPHERS

Most of the photographs in the text were taken by **Harold Davis** of Jersey City, New Jersey , whose knowledge of photography is as great as his humility is rare. He also contributed to some of the pages in the I.D.: 151, the top two of 165, the top of 173, 180-181, 183-184, the middle of 192, the big pictures of 198 and 199, 200, the top of 203, 204, the bottom of 205, 206-208.

**Merle Prosofsky** of Edmonton, Alberta, Canada deserved a medal of honour for the patience he showed in trying to make most of the I.D. informative as well as stylistically stunning.  He was also responsible for the photographs on 29, 47-48, 55, 59, 61, 110, 113-115.

**Michael Toogood** of Nassau, Bahamas filled in with the desperate, last minute, missing pieces of a puzzle too long with me; 116-117, bottom 118, 119, 140, the top two of 158, the bottom right of 159, 162, the bottom two of 165, 166, the top and the bottom of 167.

The truly poor photographs of this book were taken by a photographer who is even more of a beginner with a camera than she is with a Shell Book: 20, 29, 30, 134, 139, 142-143, 149, and the last page of the book.

# INDEX

pp.151-210 refer to photographs at the end of the book

# T

# THANK YOU

How will I find words to thank all the people who took pity on this despairing beginner? **S. PETER DANCE**, one of Britain's foremost natural historians and writers, painted me a good luck painting of a conch.

**R. TUCKER ABBOTT**, one of the world's leading conchologists, one of the great malacologists of this century, "research scientist and field collector for forty years at Harvard University, the Smithsonian Institution, and the Academy of Natural Sciences in Philadelphia" author of innumerable and indispensable texts and articles, – how my stupid, little book must have driven him insane. "She didn't even know that Gigas doesn't mean Queen???" Did he say that? Not in that tone of voice, of course. With the patience of Job, the wit of Voltaire, and the resourcefulness of Houdini, he actually read the whole book with not even a sigh of reproach as his pen corrected the worst of its glaring errors. Words to repay this kind of kingly generosity do not exist.

**MRS. WILLIAMS**, my housekeeper in Scotland, to whom my Mother taught calligraphy, in between Cooking and Ironing and Lighting coal fires dashed to the dining room table for filling in,

"Just one more page Mrs. Sandy."

Nineteen years Curator of Molluscs at the Smithsonian Institution, intrepid sailor of the high seas in search of shell treasure, **DR. HARALD A. REHDER** rallied round his friends in corals and sea eggs and crabbies, so they could make sure this crazy lady was up to date in the shifting sands of Latin names not to mention English.

My genius editor in California insisted upon a **REAL GAME** so that it would be **FUN** instead of the deathly boring subject it appeared to him and his suburbanite friends.

Finally, adding to this list my secretary **BECCY**, whose brilliance has always created Order out of Chaos, making me realize that in every staircase there is one step we never manage entirely by ourselves.

*Thank you Everyone*
*from Céline*
February, 1993